MW01291816

"This book is a gem. It sh[...]
gospel is both for our sal[...]
love our Lord and others well with our head, heart and hands. It
demonstrates that our sanctification is not an end in itself, but for
Great Commission advancement among the nations. *The Pursuit of
Holistic Holiness* will serve the Church well for many years to come.
I am delighted to commend its widest reading."

> - **Daniel L. Akin**, President, Southeastern
> Baptist Theological Seminary

"It is so good to see pastor-scholars like Dr. Tankersley write solid and
informative books on discipleship and holistic spiritual maturation.
The Pursuit of Holistic Holiness is just the thing we need at the urgent
hour. It is full of helpful, insightful wisdom on spiritual formation
accessible to a general audience. I am delighted to recommend this
book."

> - **J.P. Moreland**, Distinguished Professor of Philosophy,
> Talbot School of Theology, Biola University
> and author of *Finding Quiet*

"There are many helpful books available on spiritual formation,
but this one has become a new favorite. Dan Tankersley rightly
understands that holiness is holistic because the entire person has
been redeemed and is being conformed to the image of Jesus Christ.
*The Pursuit of Holistic Holiness: A Primer for Christian Spiritual
Formation* strikes the right balance between biblical/theological
depth and practical accessibility. This book is ideal for small
groups, church staffs, or personal devotional readings. I will be
recommending it to others for many years to come."

> - **Nathan A. Finn**, Provost / Dean of the University
> Faculty, North Greenville University

"The writer of Hebrews tells us to strive for holiness because, without it, no one will see the Lord (Hebrews 12:14), but for some reason, many Christians don't take the pursuit of holiness seriously. To make ourselves more comfortable, we mock holiness with phrases like "Holy Roller" and "Holier than thou." Sadly many modern-day Christians have become grace abusers and see holiness as legalistic. Dan Tankersley informs us in great biblical detail that the pursuit of holiness is actually obedience, not legalism."

- **Rick Burgess**, Author / Speaker and Co-Host
of *The Rick and Bubba Show*

"Welcome to the fight Dr. Dan Tankersley. Yes, there is a fight about which gospel will emerge as the dominant one among Christian leaders. Will it be a gospel that is easy to attain, impossible to lose, and invisible to the eye? In other words, a gospel that is focused on forgiveness only, attaining heaven only, by reciting words only. Or will it be the one Jesus taught, what might be called the 'Follow Me,' gospel? Where you can tell that God has saved and called them because the recipient is transformed. Dietrich Bonhoeffer said it so well, 'Faith is only real in obedience.' We all long for a day when the norm is to understand discipleship as a normal part of what it means to be saved. This really fine work by Dan Tankersley helps us all move into a more robust and consequential gospel."

- **Bill Hull**, Co-Founder, The Bonhoeffer Project,
Author of *Conversion & Discipleship: You
Can't Have One Without the Other*

"Surely every Christian has wondered at some point, 'What is God's will for my life?' While there are certainly individualized answers to that question, the general answer is the same: To be conformed into the likeness of Jesus. That transformation is not just about behavior; it is indeed a holistic holiness. I'm thankful that *The Pursuit of*

Holistic Holiness not only embraces this vision of God's will for us all, but also gives us a clear pathway to follow as we embrace God's work in and through us to this end."

– **Michael Kelley**, Sr. Vice President, Church Ministries, Lifeway Christian Resources

"Re-orienting our people towards healthy, biblical, reproducible disciple-making is critical for our collective spiritual health and essential for our collective gospel mission. *The Pursuit of Holistic Holiness* will help you and your church do just that. Dan explains the *why* of discipleship rooted in the gospel we teach and the *how* of discipleship, modeled by Christ himself. If you want a single resource to motivate you and those you lead to discipleship as well as give you the tools to start a movement of discipleship, this is it."

– **Paul A. Thompson**, Pastor, Calvary Baptist Church of Dothan, Alabama

THE PURSUIT OF
HOLISTIC HOLINESS

A Primer for
Christian Spiritual Formation

Daniel Spurgeon Tankersley

WESTBOW
PRESS®
A DIVISION OF THOMAS NELSON
& ZONDERVAN

This book is a work of non-fiction. Unless otherwise noted, the author and the publisher make no explicit guarantees as to the accuracy of the information contained in this book and in some cases, names of people and places have been altered to protect their privacy.

WestBow Press books may be ordered through booksellers or by contacting:

WestBow Press
A Division of Thomas Nelson & Zondervan
1663 Liberty Drive
Bloomington, IN 47403
www.westbowpress.com
844-714-3454

Because of the dynamic nature of the Internet, any web addresses or links contained in this book may have changed since publication and may no longer be valid. The views expressed in this work are solely those of the author and do not necessarily reflect the views of the publisher, and the publisher hereby disclaims any responsibility for them.

Any people depicted in stock imagery provided by Getty Images are models, and such images are being used for illustrative purposes only. Certain stock imagery © Getty Images.

Scripture quotations are from the ESV® Bible (The Holy Bible, English Standard Version®), copyright © 2001 by Crossway, a publishing ministry of Good News Publishers. Used by permission. All rights reserved.

ISBN: 978-1-6642-0595-6 (sc)
ISBN: 978-1-6642-0597-0 (hc)
ISBN: 978-1-6642-0596-3 (e)

Library of Congress Control Number: 2020918072

Print information available on the last page.

WestBow Press rev. date: 10/14/2020

Dedication

To Calvary Baptist Church of Dothan, Alabama

Acknowledgements

I'm grateful for my wife, Anna, who has supported me throughout this writing project. I'm thankful for Calvary Baptist Church of Dothan, Alabama. God has used Calvary more than any other church to form me in Christ. I want to thank the faculty of New Orleans Baptist Theological Seminary, especially Dr. Randy Stone, for guiding me in my understanding of discipleship and spiritual formation.

I appreciate the late Jerry Bridges and Dallas Willard for their enduring insights on spiritual formation. I'm indebted to Bill Hull, Robby Gallaty, Greg Ogden, Bobby Harrington, and Robert Coleman for their faithful teaching on discipleship and spiritual formation. I'm thankful for Dennis Hollinger, whose book *Head, Heart, & Hands* sparked my interest in holistic holiness. I'd like to thank Mike and Sue Marie Coe for their editing help. Finally, I'm grateful to God, who gave me the desire to complete this project.

Contents

Introduction

You shall be holy, for I am holy.
— 1 Peter 1:16

There are three basic goals in spiritual growth: to learn what we need to know, become what we were meant to be, and do what we were meant to do.
— Max Anders[1]

God is holy, and he intends for us to be holy (1 Pet. 1:16). Though God designs human beings to be holy, or set apart, like him (Gen. 1:26–27), humanity defiled God's holiness when Adam and Eve sinned against him in the Garden of Eden. Adam and Eve's sin corrupted humanity, and now every human is born into unholiness, evil, sin, and death. Fallen human beings still bear God's image (Js. 3:9–10), but sin distorts his image in us.

Since the fall of humanity, the highest goal of God's work in the universe is the sanctification of human beings (1 Thess. 4:3). To accomplish this work, God sent his own Son to the earth to reverse the curse of sin. Through Jesus, God makes all things new (Rev. 21:5). Through Jesus, Christians are restored to holiness. Through union with Christ, there is a holiness we already possess (Rom. 3:21–26).

---

[1] Max Anders, *Brave New Discipleship: Cultivating Scripture-Driven Christians in a Culture-Driven World* (Nashville, TN: Thomas Nelson, 2015), 123.

However, there is also a holiness we must pursue (Heb. 12:14). Peter emphasizes the pursuit of holiness, saying, "As obedient children, do not be conformed to the passions of your former ignorance, but as he who called you is holy, you also be holy in all your conduct" (1 Pet. 1:14–15). As we pursue holiness, we become who we already are in Christ.

The apostle Paul provides the framework for the pursuit of holiness by commanding the Philippians, "work out your own salvation with fear and trembling, for it is God who works in you, both to will and to work for his good pleasure"[2] (Phil. 2:12–13). Growth in holiness, also referred to as *spiritual formation*, rests ultimately in the grace of God, who works in and through the Christian. However, the Christian is required to work to grow in holiness. God commands Christians to *press on* and *strain forward* in order to increase in Christlikeness (Phil. 3:12–14).

John says that when a person is born again, he or she receives "the Spirit without measure" (Jn. 3:34). The apostle Peter verifies that upon spiritual birth, Christians receive everything they need to live a godly life (2 Pet. 1:3). Therefore, if spiritual growth is hindered in the Christian life, what's lacking is not on God's end; it's on our end. Paul tells the Ephesians, "Blessed be the God and Father of our Lord Jesus Christ, *who has blessed us in Christ with every spiritual blessing* in the heavenly places, even as he chose us in him before the foundation of the world, *that we should be holy and blameless* before him" (Eph. 1:3–4, emphasis mine).

Since all true Christians are credited with the righteousness of Christ, you could ask, "What's the big deal about avoiding the pursuit of holiness?" There is more at stake than you might realize. By neglecting holiness, you diminish the abundant life Jesus offers, you damage your relationships, you weaken your Christian witness, you impair your communion with God, and you ultimately displease

---

[2] Unless otherwise noted, all scripture citations will be from the English Standard Version.

and dishonor God. In the worst case, an ongoing neglect of holiness may reveal an illegitimate faith. God's Word frequently motivates us to pursue holiness, because as we do so, our faith is displayed, God is glorified, and we are blessed.

This book highlights the pursuit of holiness as a *holistic* endeavor, meaning spiritual formation involves the mind, heart, and hands and each component affects the others. God designed the mind, heart, and hands to work in perfect harmony with one another, but sin has thwarted that design. Too often, the Christian's growth in holiness is stifled due to an unbalanced approach.

All Christians are shaped by cultures, church backgrounds, and personalities that tend to predispose them toward a faith of the head, heart, or hands.[3] Some have a "head-only faith" that is centered on attaining knowledge. Others have a "heart-only faith" that is fueled by emotion. Still, others have a "hands-only faith" that is driven by doing good works. Taken alone, a faith of the head, heart, or hands is deeply flawed, because each represents a fragmented faith with imbalances and inadequacies.[4] A separation of the head, heart, and hands is inconsistent with God's design for Christians.

The solution to lopsided and stagnant spiritual growth is a holistic approach to holiness, centered on the Great Commandment. When asked by a scribe what the greatest commandment is, Jesus replies, "The most important is, 'Hear, O Israel: The Lord our God, the Lord is one. And you shall love the Lord your God with all your heart and with all your soul and with all your mind and with all your strength.' The second is this: 'You shall love your neighbor as yourself.' There is no other commandment greater than these" (Mk. 12:29–31). The Great Commandment, which has been called the North Star of spiritual formation, is the highest aim of the Christian

---

[3] Dennis P. Hollinger, *Head, Heart, & Hands: Bringing Together Christian Thought, Passion and Action* (Downers Grove, IL: InterVarsity Press, 2005), 190.
[4] Ibid., 32.

life.[5] Spiritual formation is about loving God with all that we are. In doing so, we progress from holistic brokenness to holistic holiness.

Book Overview

The Pursuit of Holistic Holiness begins with the gospel. The gospel is "the power of God for salvation" (Rom. 1:16) *and* the fuel for transformation. As we understand and apply the gospel to our lives, God progressively changes us into the image of Christ. Chapter One highlights the need for gospel clarity, cautions against false gospels, defines the gospel according to Jesus, surveys Paul's "gospel reminder" to the Corinthians, and concludes with a call to self-examination.

Chapter Two emphasizes sanctification as God's will for his children (1 Thess. 4:3). The gospel is a portal into a new reality of guaranteed transformation. As a result, Christian growth into maturity is always expected. This chapter defines spiritual formation, explains the "already/not yet" paradox of the Christian life, exposes God's sovereignty and human responsibility in sanctification, and highlights the world, the flesh, and the devil as "spiritual growth stoppers."

Chapter Three explores the holistic nature of spiritual formation. *Holistic* means there are interconnected parts of spiritual formation that make up the whole, and each part affects the others. Holistic spiritual formation stresses the centrality of Christ over every component of our lives (head, heart, and hands). This chapter begins by highlighting the Great Commandment and defining the *head*, *heart*, and *hands*. Next, using scripture and prominent Christian voices, Chapter Three explores the interconnectedness of the head, heart, and hands. This chapter includes case studies that caution against potential pitfalls of spiritual formation and concludes with a simple diagnostic test to help you determine your spiritual growth tendencies and susceptibilities.

---

[5] James Wilhoit, *Spiritual Formation as if the Church Mattered: Growing in Christ Through Community* (Grand Rapids, MI: Baker Academic, 2008), 45.

Chapters Four through Six explore how to pursue the mind, heart, and hands of Christ. Jesus is our standard in spiritual formation because, as the ideal human, he has the perfect mind, heart, and hands. He alone perfectly fulfills the Great Commandment. While the mind and hands of Christ are pursued directly, the heart of Christ must be pursued indirectly through spiritual disciplines.

Chapter Seven addresses the relationship between spiritual formation and discipleship, emphasizing that spiritual growth should naturally and inevitably express itself through the Great Commission. There is no greater work in the Christian life than discipleship. As the Father sent Jesus on a mission, so Jesus sends his followers on a mission (Jn. 17:18). Conformity to the image of Christ is conformity into a disciple-maker for the sake of others. God works in his people in order to work *through* his people. The Great Commandment and the Great Commission fuel one another.

Author's Purpose

Professor Klaus Issler notes that the spiritual formation process requires us to *awake* to our formation gaps, *admit* the gap with honesty and transparency, *ask* God for his formative grace, and *act* according to God's will.[6] Wherever you are in the spiritual formation process, I hope this book will facilitate your path forward. I pray this book will prime you for gospel-centered, biblical, holistic, and practical spiritual formation. I trust that God will use this book to help you faithfully pursue the Great Commandment, engage in the Great Commission, mature in Christ, and bear fruit for his glory (Col. 1:28; Jn. 15:8). In the words of the apostle Paul, "May God himself, the God of peace, sanctify you through and through. May your whole spirit, soul and body be kept blameless at the coming of our Lord Jesus Christ" (1 Thess. 5:23).

---

[6] Klaus Issler, *Living Into the Life of Jesus: The Formation of Christian Character* (Downers Grove, IL: InterVarsity Press, 2012), 55.

1
CHAPTER

The Gospel: Transforming Power Included

I am not ashamed of the gospel, for it is the power of
God for salvation to everyone who believes,…
– Romans 1:16

The gospel is not just the diving board off of which we jump
into the pool of Christianity; the gospel is the pool itself. So
keep going deeper into it. You'll never find the bottom.
– JD Greear[1]

Many self-professed Christians look nothing like Christ. They do not think like Jesus, act like Jesus, or exhibit his character traits. If salvation were only about forgiveness of sins and going to heaven after death, it would not matter much how one lives after being saved. But salvation includes much more than forgiveness of sins and going to heaven. According to scripture, genuine salvation guarantees a person's transformation into the image of Jesus himself. Therefore, salvation will always result in a changed life.

Many non-Christlike Christians are the fruit of false gospels.

---

[1] JD Greear, *Gospel: Recovering the Power that Made Christianity Revolutionary* (Nashville, TN: B&H Publishing Group, 2011), 248.

Dallas Willard, a Christian philosopher known for his writings on spiritual formation, refers to the non-Christlike Christian as a "vampire Christian." He defines a vampire Christian as a person who simply wants to use something Jesus did but has no desire for Jesus. The vampire Christian says, "I'll take a bit of your blood, Jesus—enough to cover my debts—but I'll not be staying close to you until I have to."[2] The vampire Christian's gospel, along with all other false gospels, does not lead to the salvation and transformation God intends.

As the foundation of spiritual formation, the gospel is of first importance (1 Cor. 15:1–6). The gospel is "the power of God for salvation" (Rom. 1:16) *and* the fuel for transformation. The gospel of God is the *only* means by which a person can be transformed into the image of Christ. Therefore, the pursuit of holiness requires a clear understanding of the gospel. Professor James Wilhoit notes, "All our spiritual problems come from a failure to apply the gospel…spiritual formation is first and foremost about the gospel."[3] As we understand and apply the gospel to our lives, God progressively changes us into the image of his Son.

Gospel Clarity

"What is the gospel?" may seem like a simple question, but if you ask ten people, you will likely get ten different answers. Pastor Greg Gilbert points out in his book *What Is the Gospel?* that even Christians disagree about what the gospel is.[4] Since there is a fog of confusion around the gospel, even among Christians, the most basic issue the church faces today is restoring the gospel message of God.

---

[2] Dallas Willard, *Renewing the Christian Mind: Essays, Interviews, and Talks* (New York, NY: HarperCollins Publishers, 2016), 310.

[3] James Wilhoit, *Spiritual Formation as if the Church Mattered: Growing in Christ Through Community* (Grand Rapids, MI: Baker Academic, 2008), 32.

[4] Greg Gilbert, *What Is the Gospel?* (Wheaton, IL: Crossway, 2010), 17.

Gospel clarity is an antidote to the widespread gospel confusion and false conversion of our day. Only the gospel of God has the power to create genuine and healthy followers of Jesus Christ.[5] If you do not think gospel clarity is important, consider the apostle Paul's double-curse warning against those who preach false gospels: "If anyone is preaching to you a gospel contrary to the one you received, let him be accursed" (Gal. 1:9). Paul uses the strongest possible language to warn against the greatest potential threat, false gospels. Paul understands that if we lose the true gospel, we lose the power unto salvation and transformation.

The Pharisees of Jesus's day are examples of people who distort the gospel. Jesus tells them they are like whitewashed tombs, full of deadness and impurity; they look beautiful on the outside, but their hearts are corrupt and dark (Mt. 23:27–28). The false gospel of the Pharisees does not result in inward transformation. Furthermore, as the Pharisees perpetuate their gospel of legalism, Jesus tells them they are making disciples of hell (Mt. 23:15). The New Testament is filled with warnings about false teachers and false gospels. Discipleship enthusiast Bill Hull notes, "If we get the gospel wrong, we get everything wrong. If we get the gospel right, we are on a holy and healthy journey into discipleship."[6]

The Gospel Is an Announcement

In the original Greek language, the English word *gospel* means "good news." It is found throughout the New Testament. For example, in scripture, we read of "the gospel of Jesus Christ" (Mk. 1:1), "the gospel of the kingdom" (Mt. 4:23), "the gospel of the grace of God"

---

[5] Bill Hull, *The Disciple-Making Church, Updated Edition: Leading a Body of Believers on the Journey of Faith* (Grand Rapids, MI: Baker Publishing Group, 2010), 12.

[6] Bill Hull, *Conversion and Discipleship: You Can't Have One without the Other* (Grand Rapids, MI: Zondervan, 2016), 14.

(Acts 20:24), "the gospel of the glory of Christ" (2 Cor. 4:4), "the gospel of peace" (Eph. 6:15), "an eternal gospel" (Rev. 14:6), and "the gospel of God" (Mk. 1:14). Although the gospel is described in different ways, it's the same gospel. The gospel Jesus preached is the same gospel Paul and other faithful disciples preached. There is only one true gospel.

Pastor and theologian Tim Keller helpfully distinguishes the gospel as an announcement versus advice. He says the gospel is "an announcement of something that has happened in history, something that's been done for you that changes your status forever...the essence of other religions is advice; Christianity is essentially news...the gospel is that God connects to you not on the basis of what you've done (or haven't done) but on the basis of what Jesus has done, in history, for you."[7] The gospel is essentially an announcement that comes from God himself to the world concerning the salvation available only through Jesus Christ.

The Gospel Is Simple, Yet Profound

The gospel message is so simple a child can understand it. If necessary, it can be communicated to an extent in a thirty-second elevator ride with a single Bible verse. For example: "For God so loved the world, that he gave his only Son, that whoever believes in him should not perish but have eternal life" (Jn. 3:16). "The wages of sin is death, but the free gift of God is eternal life in Christ Jesus our Lord" (Rom. 6:23). "For our sake he made him to be sin who knew no sin, so that in him we might become the righteousness of God" (2 Cor. 5:21). Although the gospel is simple, it is also profound.

The same, simple gospel a child understands can perplex the greatest philosophers. The same gospel that can be communicated in a thirty-second elevator ride cannot be exhausted by a preacher in

---

[7] Tim Keller, *Jesus the King: Understanding the Life and Death of the Son of God* (New York, NY: Penguin Group, 2011), 16–17.

thirty years. The same gospel that can be conveyed in one Bible verse is so grand and advanced it takes the entire narrative of scripture to express it. It's no wonder Peter says the angels still long to look into the things of the gospel because it amazes their minds (1 Pet. 1:12). The further into the gospel we go, the more glorious it becomes.

Jesus's Gospel of the Kingdom

There is no better way to approach the gospel than from the angle of Jesus's teaching. In their book, *The Discipleship Gospel*, Bill Hull and Ben Sobels skillfully define the gospel according to Jesus by examining Mark 1:14–17 and Mark 8:27–31. From these two passages, Hull and Sobels identify seven essential elements that provide the framework for the gospel Jesus preached.[8] Let's examine these two passages, beginning with Mark 1:14–17:

> Now after John was arrested, Jesus came into Galilee, proclaiming the gospel of God, and saying, "The time is fulfilled, and the kingdom of God is at hand; repent and believe in the gospel." Passing alongside the Sea of Galilee, he saw Simon and Andrew the brother of Simon casting a net into the sea, for they were fishermen. And Jesus said to them, "Follow me, and I will make you become fishers of men."

From this passage, Hull and Sobels identify four essential elements of the gospel Jesus preached: God's kingdom is here; repent from sin; believe the gospel; follow Jesus.[9]

---

[8] Bill Hull and Ben Sobels, *The Discipleship Gospel: What Jesus Preached—We Must Follow* (Brentwood, TN: HIM Publications, 2018), 15.
[9] Ibid., 36.

God's Kingdom Is Here (Mark 1:15)

While many people have a self-centered view of the gospel, Jesus preached a kingdom-centered gospel. The kingdom of God was the primary subject of Jesus's message and ministry. The kingdom of God is a bit mysterious because it has come, is coming, and is yet to come.[10] With this "already, but not yet" tension in mind, Hull and Sobels define the kingdom of God as "the restoration of God's rule over all things," pointing out that, "since the fall, God has been putting all things in place so that this fallen, earthly realm might be restored under his absolute sovereign rule."[11]

In Mark 1:15, Jesus inaugurates the kingdom of God by announcing that he has come to reverse the curse of sin. Greg Gilbert comments, "The rightful King of the world had come, and all that stood in the way of the establishment of his kingdom—sin, death, hell, Satan—was being decisively overcome."[12] Jesus's ministry demonstrates his authority and kingship over all things. Jesus preaches that the kingdom of God is now available in and through his life, teaching, death, and resurrection.[13] The great hope Christians have is that King Jesus will one day return to consummate his kingdom once and for all. In the meantime, we are to seek first the kingdom of God and pray, "Your kingdom come, your will be done, on earth as it is in heaven" (Mt. 6:10).

We either live in God's kingdom or in the kingdom of this world, also known as the kingdom of darkness (Col. 1:13). Satan dominates the kingdom of darkness which leads to eternal damnation. Because the kingdom of darkness is the default kingdom for all of humanity, the most important question one can ask is "How can I escape

---

[10] Hull and Sobels, 54.

[11] Ibid., 51.

[12] Gilbert, 89.

[13] Steven L. Porter, Gary W. Moon, and J.P. Moreland, *Until Christ is Formed in You: Dallas Willard and Spiritual Formation* (Abilene, TX: Abilene Christian University Press, 2018), 219.

the kingdom of darkness and enter into God's eternal kingdom of light?" Thankfully, Jesus provides a clear answer to that question. He commands us to repent from sin, believe the gospel, and follow him (Mk. 1:15–17). Entry into God's kingdom is not automatic. It requires action on our part.

Repent from Sin (Mark 1:15)

Jesus does not just proclaim that the kingdom of God has come; he calls people to respond to that proclamation by repenting. God commands all people everywhere to repent (Acts 17:30). Jesus says in Luke 13:3, "Unless you repent, you will perish." The word *repent* is an imperative that means "to reverse course," or "to turn away from something."[14] The "something" we are to turn away from is sin. Sin can be defined as "any failure to conform to the moral law of God in act, attitude, or nature."[15] Sin destroys relationships, causes us to make bad choices, causes us to desire evil things, and moves us to act in destructive ways. Sin renders us spiritually dead, and if left unforgiven, results in eternal death in hell. Sin is our most significant problem because it separates us from God. We must realize how much God hates sin, acknowledge our sin, and repent. It's worth noting that the word *repent* is a present imperative in the Greek language, which means repentance is not a one-time act. Instead, God commands us to live in a state of ongoing repentance. There is no salvation without repentance, and there is no salvation without belief.

---

[14] Keller, 15.

[15] Wayne Grudem, *Systematic Theology: An Introduction to Biblical Doctrine* (Grand Rapids, MI: Zondervan, 1994), 490.

Believe the Gospel (Mark 1:15)

As seen throughout the New Testament, repentance and belief are two sides of the single coin of salvation. In repentance, we turn away from sin. In belief, we turn to God. The word *believe* means more than simply agreeing that something might be true. Biblical belief includes faith and obedience. For example, if you were in a plane that was about to crash and a parachute was available to you, you would not just believe that parachute could save you; you would put it on and jump out of the plane before it crashed. In the same way, it is not enough to simply acknowledge that Jesus is the Savior — we must wholeheartedly trust him as if our lives depended on it…because they do! God commands us to "put on" the Lord Jesus Christ (Rom. 13:14).

The gospel declares that "God did not send his Son into the world to condemn the world, but in order that the world might be saved through him. Whoever *believes* in him is not condemned, but whoever does not believe is condemned already, because he has not believed in the name of the only Son of God" (Jn. 3:17–18, emphasis mine). All who believe in Jesus will be saved. Whoever does not believe in Jesus is condemned already. Like the word *repent*, the word *believe* is also a Greek present imperative, which means we should live in a state of ongoing belief. Repentance and belief should mark our initial conversion to Christ, but they should also mark the rest of our lives.

Follow Jesus (Mark 1:17)

The very next command Jesus gives his disciples after "repent and believe the gospel," is "follow me." Jesus says, "If anyone wishes to come after me, he must deny himself, and take up his cross and follow me" (Mk. 8:34). Christ comes with a radical message followed by a radical call to obedience. After all, a faith that is not active and fruitful is not real faith (Js. 2:17). When Jesus says, "follow me," he is saying that knowing him, loving him, becoming like him, and serving him must be the supreme desire and commitment of one's life; everything else comes second. The gospel is not about following advice; it is about following a King.[16] According to Mark 1:17, a disciple is someone who is following Jesus, being changed by Jesus, and is committed to the mission of Jesus.[17]

Jesus never teaches that a person can receive salvation and *not* follow him. He warns against such teaching. In Luke 6:46, Jesus asks the penetrating question, "Why do you call me 'Lord, Lord' and not do what I tell you?" He also says, "Not everyone who says to me, 'Lord, Lord,' will enter the kingdom of heaven, but only the one who *does the will of my Father* who is in heaven" (Mt. 7:21, emphasis mine). John echoes Jesus's warning by saying, "Whoever says 'I know him' but does not keep his commandments is a liar, and the truth is not in him, but whoever keeps his word, in him truly the love of God is perfected. By this we may know that we are in him: whoever says he abides in him ought to walk in the same way in which he walked" (1 Jn. 2:4–6). As we follow Jesus by faith, we are living in his kingdom.[18] As we follow Jesus, we remain on the narrow path that leads to life, which only a few find (Mt. 7:13–14).

Sinners are required to repent, believe, and follow Jesus. However, repentance, belief, and obedience must not be considered acts that earn salvation. Paul reminds the Ephesians, "for by grace you have been saved through faith. And this is not your own doing; it is a gift of God, not a result of works, so that no one may boast" (Eph. 2:8–9). No person is saved because of their works. Pastor John Piper comments on this text, "grace is God's free giving, and faith is our helpless receiving. When God justifies us by faith alone, he has

---

[16] Keller, 22.

[17] Bobby Harrington and Jim Putman, *DiscipleShift: Five Steps That Help Your Church to Make Disciples Who Make Disciples* (Grand Rapids, MI: Zondervan, 2013), 51.

[18] Hull and Sobels, 53.

respect not to faith as a virtue but faith as a receiving of Christ. So it is the same as saying that not our virtue, but Christ's virtue, is the ground of our justification."[19] Therefore, as we repent, believe, and follow Jesus, we do not earn salvation; rather, we demonstrate the reality of God's saving grace in our lives.

Now that we have defined the first four elements of the gospel Jesus preached, let's read Mark 8:27–31 to find the other three elements:

> And Jesus went on with his disciples to the villages of Caesarea Philippi. And on the way he asked his disciples, "Who do people say that I am?" And they told him, "John the Baptist; and others say, Elijah; and others, one of the prophets." And he asked them, "But who do you say that I am?" Peter answered him, "You are the Christ." And he strictly charged them to tell no one about him. And he began to teach them that the Son of Man must suffer many things and be rejected by the elders and the chief priests and the scribes and be killed, and after three days rise again.

Hull and Sobels identify three more gospel elements from this passage: Jesus is the Christ; Jesus died for our sins; Jesus was resurrected.[20]

Jesus Is the Christ (Mark 8:29)

To profess Jesus as "the Christ," as Peter does, is to proclaim Jesus as the anointed one about whom all Scripture had been written.

---

[19] John Piper, *Think: The Life of the Mind and the Love of God* (Wheaton, IL: Crossway, 2010), 71.
[20] Hull and Sobels, 39.

Jesus is the long-awaited, prophesied Savior of the Old Testament. Hull and Sobels explain, "the title 'Christ' invokes the weight of the entire Old Testament, indeed all Scripture. It's one word that encapsulates all of the Bible's teachings about God's promised savior and everything that the Bible reveals about Jesus…to confess Jesus as 'Christ' was to declare that he was God's anointed one, the king of God's kingdom…God's anointed king."[21]

Jesus Died for our Sins (Mark 8:31)

The Bible says all people have sinned, and the wages of sin is death (Rom. 3:23; 6:23). The punishment for sin is not just physical death, but eternal death in a place called *hell*. Sin separates people from Holy God, but the good news is that "God shows his love for us in that while we were still sinners, Christ died for us" (Rom. 5:8). John says, "By this we know love, that he [Jesus] laid down his life for us" (1 Jn. 3:16). Jesus lovingly and sacrificially took the punishment for our sin by enduring torture and eventual death on the cross. But Jesus's death is not the end of the story.

Jesus was Resurrected (Mark 8:31)

After Jesus was dead for three days, he rose from the grave. Jesus was resurrected (1 Cor. 15:20)! The resurrection is the linchpin of the gospel. Sin, death, and hell cannot be defeated without the resurrection. The apostle Paul says if Jesus was not raised, then preaching the gospel is futile, faith in Jesus is in vain, we are still in our sins, and we should be pitied (1 Cor. 15:14–19).

Salvation requires belief in the resurrection. Paul says, "if you confess with your mouth that Jesus is Lord and *believe in your heart that God raised him from the dead*, you will be saved" (Rom. 10:9,

---

[21] Hull and Sobels, 61.

emphasis mine). Tim Keller notes the essence of the gospel is that "Jesus died and rose again so that all his followers could, eventually, do the same."[22] Not only was Jesus resurrected, but one day all of his followers will receive glorified bodies as they are resurrected to an eternal New Heaven and New Earth (1 Cor. 15:50–56; Rev. 21).

A Gospel Definition

Now that we have identified and explained the seven elements of the gospel Jesus preached, let's combine these elements with other truths from scripture for a gospel definition. We are not redefining the gospel. Rather, we are choosing biblical language to express the gospel according to Jesus.[23] The gospel can be defined as follows:

> The kingdom of God has come through Jesus. He is Christ, the King, God's only Son. He lived a perfect life, died on the cross for our sins, was buried, and was resurrected on the third day according to the scriptures. God, our loving and graceful Father, saves everyone who repents from their sin, believes the gospel, and follows Jesus in the power of the Holy Spirit. When King Jesus returns on the last day, the Great Day of Judgment, all Christians will enter the eternal kingdom of God (Mk. 1:14–17; 8:27–31; 1 Cor. 15:1–5; Jn. 3:16; Eph. 2:8–10; Mt. 25:31–46).[24]

While this gospel definition could be expanded, shortened, or modified, it represents the fundamental message of the gospel. The gospel defined above is the same gospel that turned the world upside

---

[22] Keller, xiii.

[23] Hull and Sobels, 112.

[24] Adapted from page 109 of *The Discipleship Gospel*.

down over two thousand years ago (Acts 17:6). The gospel message is foolishness to those who are perishing, but it is the power of God to those being saved (1 Cor. 1:18).

Jesus says, "This gospel of the kingdom will be proclaimed throughout the whole world as a testimony to all nations, and then the end will come" (Mt. 24:14). If we proclaim the wrong gospel, our work on earth will not be completed. If we alter the gospel, we remove its power. Therefore, we should aim to "contend for the faith once for all delivered to the saints" (Jude 1:3). While we cannot expose every false gospel in this short book,[25] we should adhere to the words of Charles Spurgeon, who said, "Let the pure gospel go forth in all its lion-like majesty, and it will soon clear its own way and ease itself of its adversaries."[26]

Paul's Gospel Reminder

The apostle Paul is a man who perpetuated the pure gospel. When Paul hears the church he planted in Corinth is experiencing division, jealousy, strife, worldliness, pride, immorality, idolatry, disobedience, and a lack of love for God and others, he reinforces the gospel to them. After writing about spiritual gifts, love, and orderly worship, Paul writes:

> Now I would remind you, brothers, of the gospel I preached to you, which you received, in which you stand, and by which you are being saved, if you hold fast to the word I preached to you—unless you believed in vain. For I delivered to you as of first importance what I also received: that Christ died

---

[25] To identify prominent false gospels in the American culture, I highly recommend Bill Hull's *Conversion & Discipleship*.

[26] Spurgeon said this in a sermon titled "The Lover of God's Law Filled with Peace" on January 2nd, 1888.

> for our sins in accordance with the Scriptures, that
> he was buried, that he was raised on the third day in
> accordance with the Scriptures,… (1 Cor. 15:1–4)

Right away, we see that what Paul shares with the Corinthians is nothing new; he shares a "reminder" of what had already been shared with them before. Paul reminds them of the gospel that led to their salvation, the gospel in which they "stand" and by which they are "being saved."

Paul continues verse 2 with a qualifying phrase, "if you hold fast to the word I preached to you—unless you believed in vain." This phrase does not mean that true believers are in danger of losing their salvation. Rather, Paul is warning the Corinthians about a false, or illegitimate faith. The New Living Translation of the Bible words 1 Corinthians 15:2 as follows: "It is this Good News that saves you if you continue to believe the message I told you—unless, of course, you believed something that was never true in the first place." Some of the Corinthians were holding fast to the gospel Paul preached, showing evidence of genuine salvation while others lacked genuine faith because they "believed something that was never true in the first place." Some of the Corinthians strayed away from the true faith and did not obey God because they believed a false gospel. If you profess faith in a false gospel, Paul says, "you believe in vain."

In 1 Corinthians 15:3–4, Paul reiterates that the gospel is of first importance. Then he reminds the Corinthians of the core gospel message, "that Christ died for our sins in accordance with the Scriptures, that he was buried, that he was raised on the third day in accordance with the Scriptures…" Paul's gospel was not man-made. Paul says in verse 3 that he "received" this gospel. Who did he receive it from? Paul answers, "For I would have you know, brothers, that the gospel that was preached by me is not man's gospel. For I did not receive it from any man, nor was I taught it, but *I received it through a revelation of Jesus Christ*" (Gal. 1:11–12, emphasis mine) Paul received this gospel from Jesus Christ himself.

So, it's no wonder Paul reinforces the same gospel Jesus preached; there is only one true gospel.

The Sustaining Gospel

Throughout his letters, Paul emphasizes that the gospel saves *and* sustains the believer. While many Christians think the gospel should be preached only to non-Christians, Paul frequently preaches the gospel to *believers* to encourage and strengthen them in the faith. For example, he tells the Colossians, "So then, just as you received Christ Jesus as Lord, continue to live your lives in him, rooted and built up in him, strengthened in the faith as you were taught" (Col. 2:6,7). He sarcastically asks the Galatians if they think they can graduate from the gospel, saying, "Are you so foolish? Having begun by the Spirit, are you now being perfected by the flesh?" (Gal. 3:3). Paul refutes the idea that we receive the gospel, past tense, and then sustain ourselves.[27] For Paul, the gospel is not just a call to saving faith, but a call to continue in a daily walk of faith, enabling transformation.

JD Greear states, "The angels have seen God face-to-face, and yet they still can't get enough of the gospel! Do we really think we are ready to move on to something else?"[28] The gospel should inform, compel, and energize everything we do. The gospel is good news for our past, it continues to be good news for the present, and it will remain good news for all eternity.[29] As we grow in maturity, we never grow beyond our need for the gospel. The goal of spiritual formation

---

[27] Jared Wilson, *The Gospel-Driven Church: Uniting Church Growth Dreams with the Metrics of Grace* (Grand Rapids, MI: Zondervan, 2019), 85.

[28] Greear, 22.

[29] Jonathan K. Dodson, *Gospel-Centered Discipleship* (Wheaton, Ill: Crossway, 2012), 11.

is to be transformed by the gospel and to apply the gospel to all of life. Therefore, we should preach the gospel to ourselves daily.[30]

Saved: Justified, Sanctified, and Glorified

Biblical salvation is a process of justification, sanctification, and glorification. Therefore, we are, in a sense, "being saved" as Paul describes in 1 Corinthians 15:2. If a person has placed his faith in Christ, he *has been* justified, he *is being* sanctified, and he *will be* glorified.

Justified

Paul says, "those whom he predestined he also called, and those whom he called he also *justified*, and those whom he justified he also glorified" (Rom. 8:30, emphasis mine). Justification can be defined as "an instantaneous legal act of God in which he (1) thinks of our sins as forgiven and Christ's righteousness as belonging to us, and (2) declares us to be righteous in his sight."[31] Justification comes through faith (Rom. 5:1), and it is a gift from God (Rom. 3:24) grounded in the death of Christ (Rom. 5:9) apart from works (Rom. 4:5).

Sanctified

God's will for you is your sanctification (1 Thess. 4:3). The term *sanctification* can be used in the definitive sense or the progressive sense. *Definitive sanctification* refers to a Christian's decisive

---

[30] Jerry Bridges, *The Discipline of Grace* (Colorado Springs, CO: NavPress, 2006), 45.

[31] Grudem, 723.

break with, or separation from, sin as a ruling power.[32] *Progressive sanctification*, which is the focus of this book, can be defined as a "work of God and man that makes us more and more free from sin and like Christ in our actual lives."[33] God purifies believers through sanctification as a blacksmith purifies metal through smelting. Smelting is a process in which metal is repeatedly heated so that the impurities are removed. The smelting process increases the purity and value of the metal. The Old Testament prophets frequently used smelting imagery to describe God's cleansing of his people (Is. 1:25; Mal. 3:3; Jer. 9:7).

The gospel calls people to come to Jesus as they are, but it guarantees that God will not leave people as they are. When the Holy Spirit indwells a person, he guarantees change from the inside out (2 Cor. 3:18). While justification is entirely the work of God, the Christian has an indispensable role in the sanctification process, which will be addressed in the next chapter.

Glorified

When a person enters the Lord's presence, Hebrews 12:23 confirms his or her spirit will be made perfect, and the transformation process will be complete.[34] The completion of salvation is referred to as *glorification*, which can be defined as "the final step in the application of redemption. It will happen when Christ returns and raises from the dead the bodies of all believers for all time who have died, and reunites them with their souls, and changes the bodies of all believers who remain alive, thereby giving all believers at the

---

[32] Jerry Bridges, *The Gospel For Real Life: Turn to the Liberating Power of the Cross...Every Day* (Colorado Springs, CO: NavPress, 2003), 158.

[33] Grudem, 746.

[34] Jerry Bridges, *The Transforming Power of the Gospel* (Colorado Springs, CO: NavPress, 2012), 11.

same time perfect resurrection bodies like his own."[35] God promises through the gospel not only to begin a work in us, but to finish it. The day we are glorified will be the final victorious defeat of sin and death (1 Cor. 15:54–55)!

God Will Complete what He Begins

Justification, sanctification, and glorification are inseparable. Paul remarks in his letter to the Philippians, "He who began a good work in you will carry it on to completion" (Phil. 1:6). In other words, if God justifies a person, he will also sanctify and glorify the person. Sanctification is glorification begun, and glorification will be sanctification completed.[36] Jesus is the only One who can deliver us from the penalty of sin, providing our justification. He is the only One who can deliver us from the power of sin, ensuring our sanctification. And he is the only One who can deliver us from the presence of sin, promising our future glorification.[37]

Examine Yourself

God wants his children to enjoy the assurance of salvation (1 Jn. 5:13; Rom. 8:31–39). Scottish theologian Sinclair Ferguson notes, "the promises of the gospel would be emptied of their power if we had no confidence in the God who makes them and whose character is expressed in them. We would end up doubting (as Satan surely wants us to) that God is our own heavenly Father."[38] Jesus

---

[35] Grudem, 829.

[36] Maurice Roberts, *The Great Transformation: The Sanctification and Glorification of the Believer* (Carlisle, PA: Banner of Truth Trust, 2019), 1.

[37] Daniel Akin, *Exalting Jesus in Mark* (Nashville, TN: B&H Publishing Group, 2014), 39.

[38] Sinclair Ferguson, *Maturity: Growing Up and Going On in the Christian Life* (Carlisle, PA: Banner of Truth Trust, 2019), 58.

preaches on the subject of true and false conversions relentlessly and repeatedly because he doesn't want anyone to be self-deceived. He speaks of wheat and tares, good fish and rotten fish, sheep and goats, etc. In the parable of the sower (Mt. 13:3–23), one of his longest parables, Jesus describes true and false conversions by describing four types of people who hear the gospel:

1. The first hearer does not truly understand the gospel and therefore does not respond.
2. The second hearer responds to the gospel with joy, but only temporarily; as soon as life gets difficult, this so-called "convert" walks away from the faith.
3. The third hearer falls away due to worldly concerns and a desire for wealth.
4. The fourth hearer understands, believes, follows, and produces genuine fruit.

Jesus explains that only the fourth type of hearer is saved; the others may have had some sort of religious experience, but they are not genuinely converted. The fourth hearer understands, believes, follows, and bears fruit.

True believers persevere to the end and bear fruit, proving they are genuine disciples of Jesus (Mt. 24:13; Jn. 15:8). Once again, if one is truly justified, he will be sanctified and glorified. John, inspired by God, describes a genuine believer as someone who loves fellow believers and the local church because he loves God (1 Jn. 5:1), desires fellowship with God (1 Jn. 1:6–7; 5:1), follows Jesus by walking in the light of truth (1 Jn. 1:6), obeys God out of love for him (5:2–3), is eager to confess and repent from sin (1 Jn. 1:9), and considers God's grace as costly (1 Jn. 1:7, 10).

Interestingly, the Bible never instructs us to look back on any act we performed in the past to find assurance of salvation. Instead, God instructs us to examine ourselves today to see if we are in the faith (2 Cor. 13:5). Where does this chapter find you? Are you resting in the finished work of Jesus for salvation? Is the Holy Spirit testifying with your spirit that you are God's child (Rom. 8:16)? Are you repenting from sin, believing in Jesus and following him daily (Mk. 1:15–17)? Is there any good fruit in your life (Mt. 7:17)? Do you see evidence of God responding to your prayers (Mt. 21:22; Jn. 15:7)?

Now that we have established the gospel according to Jesus, in the next chapter we will examine the topic of sanctification, which is God's will for you. If Christ is in you, you *will* grow in holiness.

DISCUSSION QUESTIONS:

Why is the gospel of first importance?

What gospel did Jesus preach?

Can you trace the gospel you believe back to the gospel Jesus preached? Would Jesus recognize your gospel?

Do you know the gospel well enough to share it? Are you sharing it?

What are some common excuses for not sharing the gospel?

What "false gospels" should we be cautious of?

Is salvation a one-time event? Explain.

How can a person find assurance of salvation?

2
CHAPTER

Sanctification: God's Will for You

When one turns to the Lord, the veil is removed. Now the Lord
is the Spirit, and where the Spirit of the Lord is, there is freedom.
And we all, with unveiled face, beholding the glory of the Lord,
are being transformed into the same image from one degree of
glory to another. For this comes from the Lord who is the Spirit.
– 2 Corinthians 3:16–18

The goal of the Christian life could be summarized as our being
formed, conformed, and transformed into the image of Christ.
– Richard Foster[1]

T he gospel is a portal into a new reality of spiritual transformation.
According to 2 Corinthians 3:16–18, when a person turns to
Jesus, the veil of spiritual blindness is removed, the Lord's glory
is beheld, and transformation begins. Just as human beings are not
born as physically mature adults, neither are they "born again"
as spiritually mature adults (Jn. 3:1–21). Thus, spiritual formation

---

[1] Jeffrey Greenman and George Kalantzis, eds., *Life in the Spirit: Spiritual
Formation in Theological Perspective* (Downers Grove, IL: InterVarsity Press,
2010), 25.

is a process. Newborn Christians must gradually become mature spiritual adults, just as newborn babies gradually become physically mature adults.

Thankfully, God gives us all the resources we need for radical spiritual growth. When a person is born again, God indwells him or her with "the Spirit without measure" (Jn. 3:34). The apostle Peter says that upon spiritual birth, a person receives everything he or she needs to live a godly life (2 Pet. 1:3). So, if radical change is missing, what's lacking is not on God's end; it's on *our* end. Sadly, we often hinder our growth by neglecting to fully trust, submit to, and obey God.

We are aware something is wrong if a flower, a tree, or a child does not grow and develop. Similarly, if a Christian doesn't develop and mature as God intends, something is wrong. Professor Richard Lovelace refers to the deficiency of Christian maturity as the "sanctification gap."[2] The sanctification gap represents the missing element of life change for the believer that scripture describes.[3] George Gallup, a trusted pioneer of survey sampling, confirms the modern sanctification gap when he says, "We find there is very little difference in ethical behavior between churchgoers and those who are not active religiously...The levels of lying, cheating, and stealing are remarkably similar in both groups."[4] The purpose of this book is to help remedy the sanctification gap described by Lovelace. God has given us all we need to be holy; now, we must faithfully pursue holiness (2 Pet. 1:1–9; 3:18). If we minimize or neglect our responsibility, our spiritual growth will be hindered.

---

[2] Richard Lovelace, *Dynamics of Spiritual Life: An Evangelical Theology of Renewal* (Downers Grove, IL: InterVarsity Academic, 1979), 229–237.
[3] Alan Andrews, ed., *The Kingdom Life: A Practical Theology of Discipleship and Spiritual Formation* (Colorado Springs, CO: NavPress, 2010),143.
[4] Robby Gallaty, *Firmly Planted: How to Cultivate a Faith Rooted in Christ* (Nashville, TN: B&H Publishing Group, 2015), 67.

Spiritual Formation

God predestined all believers to be conformed into the image of his Son, Jesus Christ (Rom. 8:9). The process toward Christlikeness can be referred to as *sanctification*. Jesus pleaded to the Father for the sanctification of *all* Christians (Jn. 17:17). The sanctification process can also be called *spiritual formation*.[5] Spiritual formation is "a process of being conformed to the image of Christ for the sake of others."[6] The spiritual formation process begins at spiritual birth (Jn. 3:3–5) and continues until one dies and enters the presence of the Lord. We will focus on spiritual formation being "for the sake of others" in Chapter Seven. For now, we will approach spiritual formation with the end goal in mind: Christlikeness.

The apostle Paul was adamant that Christians become "mature in Christ" through the transforming power of the gospel (Col. 1:28). He tells the Galatians that he agonizes in the labor of ministry until Christ is formed in them (Gal. 4:19). He encourages the Corinthians by reminding them of the reality of their transformation; he tells them not to lose heart because "though [their] outer self is wasting away, [their] inner self is being renewed day by day" (2 Cor. 4:16). There is no greater promise or pursuit in life than Christlikeness.

The Already/Not Yet Paradox

As we proceed to examine spiritual formation, we should acknowledge the *already/not yet* tension of the Christian faith.[7] As Christians, we live in the *already* while we await the *not yet*. The letter of Ephesians

---

[5] Because of their intimate relationship, I will use the terms *spiritual formation*, *sanctification*, *transformation*, and *holiness* interchangeably.

[6] Robert Mulholland as cited in Evan Howard, *A Guide to Christian Spiritual Formation: How Scripture, Spirit, Community, and Mission Shape Our Souls* (Grand Rapids, MI: Baker Academic, 2018), 16.

[7] Gallaty, 42.

frequently points to this tension. As the church, we are already the fullness of Christ (1:23), and yet we long to be filled with the fullness of Christ (3:19) as we seek the measure of the stature of the fullness of Christ (4:13). As the church, we are already under our head, Christ (1:22–23), and yet we are to grow up into Christ, who is the head (4:15). As the church, we are already one, united in Christ (2:12–22), and yet we are to be eager to maintain the unity of the Spirit (4:3). We are already holy (2:19–22), and yet we walk in holiness and increase in holiness. The church is a community of God's people living in the already and not yet.[8]

The transformation, or metamorphosis, of a caterpillar into a butterfly may help us better understand the already/not yet tension of Christianity. Authors Bill Thrall and Bruce McNicol explain:

> Sometimes when we lose our grip on who God has made us to be, we must remember the butterfly... If we brought a caterpillar to a biologist and asked him to analyze it and describe its DNA, he would tell us, 'I know this looks like a caterpillar to you, but scientifically...this is fully and completely a butterfly'...The caterpillar matures into what is already true about it...So it is with us. God has given us the DNA of godliness...And now He is asking us to join Him in what He knows is true.[9]

In the same way a caterpillar is already, but not yet a butterfly, Christians are already, but not yet holy. Like the transformation of a caterpillar into a butterfly, the Christian experiences transformation of his entire being "from one degree of glory to another" (2 Cor. 3:18).

One day when Christ returns or calls us home we will be like

---

[8] Christopher Morgan, ed., *Biblical Spirituality* (Wheaton, IL: Crossway, 2019), 33–34.

[9] Andrews, 73–74.

him (1 Jn. 3:2), and the work God began in us will be complete (Rom. 8:29–30). Until that day, we must put forth the effort to become who we already are in Christ. Our responsibility is to close the gap that separates who we are in Christ from how we reflect Christ. We must "put off" the old self and "put on" the new self, as Paul tells the Ephesians (Eph. 4:22–24). Kenneth Boa, author of *Conformed to His Image*, captures the *already/not yet* tension in the way he defines spiritual formation: "Spiritual Formation is the lifelong process of becoming in our character and actions the new creations we already are in Christ. (2 Cor. 5:17); it is the working out of what God has already worked in us. (Phil. 2:12–13)"[10] The abundant life Jesus came to give is found by knowing who we are in him and living accordingly; that's the essence of spiritual formation.

A Lifelong Journey

The Christian journey is an intentional and continual commitment to a *lifelong* process of growth toward Christlikeness.[11] In a culture that longs for instant gratification and immediate results, we should understand that sanctification is a slow process that cannot be rushed. Bill Hull notes, "The formation of character into the person of Christ can't be hurried. It is a slow work, and it can get very messy. People fail, delay, make mistakes, resist, and are afraid. It is a slow work, so it can't be hurried; but it is an urgent work, so it cannot be delayed."[12] In scripture, maturity doesn't happen in a month, a year, or even a decade. Rather, scripture presents transformation as a lifelong journey of one's renewal (2 Cor. 4:16–18).

The Bible uses images of spiritual formation that emphasize

---

[10] Kenneth Boa, *Conformed to His Image* (Grand Rapids, MI: Zondervan, 2001), 257.

[11] Robert Mulholland, *Invitation to a Journey: A Road Map for Spiritual Formation* (Downers Grove, IL: InterVarsity Press, 2016), 27.

[12] Andrews, 112.

the gradual but inevitable changes that mark the Christian life.[13] A recurring image for spiritual formation in scripture is plants that are well-nourished. For example, Jeremiah 17:7–8 states:

> Blessed is the man who trusts in the Lord, whose trust is the Lord. He is like a tree planted by water, that sends out its roots by the stream, and does not fear when heat comes, for its leaves remain green, and is not anxious in the year of drought, for it does not cease to bear fruit.

Sinclair Ferguson cleverly observes, "The only plant in Scripture that grew up overnight was Jonah's castor-oil plant, and it withered the next day (Jon. 4:6–7)!"[14] Another metaphor scripture uses to demonstrate slow growth is a race. In 1 Corinthians, Paul likens the Christian life to a race in which we are runners (1 Cor. 9:24). The race is not a sprint, nor even a marathon, but a lifelong journey. Our goal is to be able to say at the end of our lives, "I have finished the race" (2 Tim. 4:7). Until then, God commands us to "run with endurance" (Heb. 12:1).

These long-duration images should shift our expectations from the fast to the slow, from the immediate to the gradual. Jesus says, "the one who endures to the end will be saved" (Mt. 10:22). Psalm 92:12 and 14 declare, "The righteous flourish like the palm tree and grow like a cedar in Lebanon...They still bear fruit in old age; they are ever full of sap and green." Perseverance is a basic expectation of Christian living. Continuing in the faith is as important as beginning in the faith.[15] Regarding spiritual formation, the journey is the destination.

---

[13] James Wilhoit, *Spiritual Formation as if the Church Mattered: Growing in Christ Through Community* (Grand Rapids, MI: Baker Academic, 2008), 24.
[14] Sinclair Ferguson, *Maturity: Growing Up and Going On in the Christian Life* (Carlisle, PA: Banner of Truth Trust, 2019), 41.
[15] Ferguson, 191.

God's Sovereignty Over Sanctification

God is in complete control of all things, including spiritual formation. All spiritual formation originates and ends with God, who is reconciling the world to himself through Christ (2 Cor. 5:18–20). What God began at justification, *he* will complete through sanctification and glorification. God's sovereignty over spiritual growth is obvious in scripture. For example, Paul tells the Corinthians, "I planted, Apollos watered, but *God gave the growth.* So neither he who plants nor he who waters is anything, but only God who gives the growth" (1 Cor. 3:6–7, emphasis mine). God sovereignly uses three primary means to transform Christians: his Spirit, his Word, and his people (the church).

God Uses His Spirit to Transform Us

The ancient Israelites continually failed God due to their hard hearts. As a result, God promises through the prophet Ezekiel, "I will give you a new heart and put a new spirit in you; I will remove from you your heart of stone and give you a heart of flesh. And I will put my Spirit in you and move you to follow my decrees and be careful to keep my laws" (Ezek. 36:26–27). Like the ancient Israelites, Christians need a power greater than their own for transformation into the image of Christ.

When Jesus speaks to his disciples in the Upper Room the night before he dies, he promises them a helper will be *with* them and in them after his departure (Jn. 14:17). That promise, along with Ezekiel's prophecy, is fulfilled when the Holy Spirit arrives at Pentecost (Acts 2). The *Holy* Spirit is a person, not a force, who indwells Christians and enables us to be *holy*. In the matter of Christian transformation, the writers of scripture sometimes speak of God's working in us and at other times of Christ's working in us. However, in all cases, it's the role of the Holy Spirit to apply and work out in our lives that which comes from God through Christ.[16] Theologian Gordon Fee explains the role of the Holy Spirit as follows:

> The Spirit searches all things (1 Cor. 2:10), knows the mind of God (1 Cor. 2:11), teaches the content of the gospel to believers (1 Cor. 2:13), dwells among or within believers (Rom. 8:11; 1 Cor. 3:16; 2 Tim. 1:14); accomplishes all things (1 Cor. 2:11), gives life to those who believe (2 Cor. 3:6), cries out from within our hearts (Gal. 4:6), leads us in the ways of God (Rom. 8:14; Gal. 5:18), bears witness with our own spirits (Rom. 8:16), has desires that are in opposition to the flesh (Gal. 5:17), helps us in our weakness (Rom. 8:26), intercedes on our behalf (Rom. 8:26–27), works all things together for our ultimate good (Rom. 8:28), strengthens believers (Eph. 3:16) and is grieved by our sinfulness (Eph. 4:30).[17]

The people of God are people commanded to display the fruit of the Spirit by walking in the Spirit, being led by the Spirit, and being filled with the Spirit (Gal. 5:16; Rom. 8:14; Eph. 5:18).

When Paul says in 2 Corinthians 3:18 that Christians are "being transformed" by "the Lord, who is the Spirit," the verb *being transformed* is passive. In other words, transformation is something being done *to* us, not *by* us.[18] We are the object, not the agent of transformation. The agent of transformation is the Holy Spirit.[19] The

---

[16] Jerry Bridges, *The Transforming Power of the Gospel* (Colorado Springs, CO: NavPress, 2012), 90.

[17] Greenman and Kalantzis, 41.

[18] Jerry Bridges, *The Discipline of Grace* (Colorado Springs, CO: NavPress, 2006), 106.

[19] Bridges, *The Transforming Power of the Gospel*, 89.

power is his, so there's no room for our boasting (Eph. 3:20–21). God fills Christians with his Spirit to accomplish his plan (2 Cor. 4:7). Spiritual formation without the Holy Spirit is impossible.

God Uses His Word to Transform Us

God tells the Israelites, "man does not live by bread alone, but man lives by every word that comes from the mouth of the Lord" (Deut. 8:3). Knowing the power of God's Word to transform, Jesus prays to the Father, "Sanctify them by the truth; your word is truth" (Jn. 17:17). David Powlison explains, "Scripture and God work in harmony...In Scripture, God comes in person. We participate by hearing and responding."[20] God's Word sanctifies us by renewing our minds (Rom. 12:2), teaching, reproofing, correcting, and training us in righteousness (2 Tim. 3:16–17), illuminating God's path for us (Ps. 119:105), sustaining us (Mt. 4:4), discerning the thoughts and intentions of our hearts (Heb. 4:12), giving us stability (Eph. 4:12–15), and enabling spiritual maturity (1 Pet. 2:2–3). God's Word is living and active (Heb. 4:12), sweeter than honey (Ps. 19:10), more precious than gold (Ps. 19:10), perfect and trustworthy (Ps. 19:7), and true (Ps. 19:9).

Evangelist D.L. Moody famously said, "The Bible was not given for our information but our transformation." Psalm 1:1–3 offers us a glimpse of a person being transformed by God's Word:

> Blessed is the man who walks not in the counsel of
> the wicked, nor stands in the way of sinners, nor sits
> in the seat of scoffers; but his delight is in the law
> of the Lord, and on his law he meditates day and
> night. He is like a tree planted by streams of water

---

[20] David Powlison, *How Does Sanctification Work?* (Wheaton, IL: Crossway, 2017), 65.

that yields its fruit in its season, and its leaf does not
wither. In all that he does, he prospers.

Pastor Brian Hedges comments, "Here is someone who is *sanctified*—
who doesn't walk in the counsel of the wicked, stand in the way of
sinners, or sit in the seat of scoffers. The person is also *satisfied*—
'blessed' or happy, and delighting in the law of the Lord. More than
that, this person, like a fruitful tree with leaves that do not wither,
is *sustained*."[21] God's Word sanctifies, satisfies, and sustains! As we
intake the Word, we put ourselves in a position to be transformed
by God.

God Uses His People (the church) to Transform Us

In addition to using his Spirit and his Word, God also uses his
people (the church) to transform us into the image of Christ. God's
Trinitarian nature is relational, so he naturally creates people to live
as relational creatures, in relationship with him and other people.
Godly growth is repeatedly mediated through people. Proverbs 27:17
states, "Iron sharpens iron, and one man sharpens another." In other
words, people are divine instruments in God's hands that he uses to
sanctify us. We would be wise to consider how God uses each person
in our path to sanctify us. God can use any person to impact us, but
the focus of this section is on how he uses the church to change us.
Diane Chandler, a professor of spiritual formation, says, "God has
hardwired us to walk through life together…in the body of Christ,
the church, in order to fashion us increasingly into the image of God
through the relational formation."[22]

---

[21] Brian Hedges, *Christ Formed in You: The Power of the Gospel for Personal
Change* (Wapwallopen, PN: Shepherd Press, 2010), 194.

[22] Jody Dean and Hal Stewart, eds., *Together We Equip: Integrating Discipleship
and Ministry Leadership for Holistic Spiritual Formation* (Bloomington, IN:
WestBow Press, 2018), 7.

God's intention to use other people to transform us is in direct opposition to the rampant individualism and isolationism of our culture. To pursue spiritual growth alone is foolishness, and it ultimately misses the point of being part of the body of Christ. Without community, spiritual formation becomes individualistic and self-centered. Community is emphasized and commanded throughout the biblical narrative; it is never presented as optional. Granted, there is a personal dimension of our spiritual growth, but there is also an indispensable corporate dimension. God's people throughout scripture didn't see themselves only as individuals participating in a faith community; instead, they viewed their individual stories in the context of the community God was redeeming.

While there are New Testament texts that describe the individual, New Testament scholar Darrell Bock observes, "Interestingly, it's the community that is described...more often than the individual. For God, it is our position together and our task together that stands at the core of spiritual formation."[23] Paul tells the Corinthians, "For in one Spirit we were all baptized into one body—Jews or Greeks, slaves or free—and all were made to drink of one Spirit" (1 Cor. 12:13). The same Spirit who joins the church to Christ also joins its members to one another.[24]

Paul explains to the Corinthians that each of them has been given a spiritual gift(s) "for the common good" (1 Cor. 12–14), highlighting that each Christian is part of the greater whole of a local body of believers. He also explains to them that if one part of the body suffers, every part suffers with it. If one part is honored, every part is honored (1 Cor. 12:26). Our spiritual growth is not just about us; it's about the edification of the entire body of Christ and the

---

[23] Paul Pettit, ed., *Foundations of Spiritual Formation: A Community Approach to Becoming Like Jesus* (Grand Rapids, MI: Kregel Publications, 2008), 108–109.

[24] John Koessler, *True Discipleship: The Art of Following Jesus* (Chicago, IL: Moody, 2003), 181.

glory of God. Author Paul Pettit concludes, "The goal of my spiritual growth is not my own individual growth *apart from* the body, but my maturity and development *within* the body and *for* the body."[25]

A Christian's faith may be personal, but it should not be private. The New Testament references at least thirty-two different "one another" commands. For example, Christians should love one another (Jn. 13:34), honor one another (Rom. 12:10), serve one another (Gal. 5:13), submit to one another (Eph. 5:21), instruct one another (Rom. 15:14), pray for one another (Js. 5:16), encourage one another (1 Thess. 4:18), and so on. These "one another" commands cannot be fulfilled in isolation. Thus, biblical community is required for our transformation.

In addition to the three primary means of his Spirit, his Word, and his church, God uses other means such as suffering, failure, success, time, and discipline to transform us. Because there is no wasted circumstance or event in the Christian life, we should view all of life as an opportunity for spiritual growth. The antidote to our pride and self-sufficiency is to remember our helplessness to change ourselves and go to the Father in humble dependence and prayer. God is sovereign over our transformation, so he gets the glory for it.

Human Responsibility in Sanctification

The obvious follow-up question to the fact that God is sovereign over our transformation is, "does that mean I have no responsibility in the transformation process?" God would give an emphatic "no" to that question. Jerry Bridges observes, "There is not a single instance in the New Testament teaching on holiness where we are taught to depend on the Holy Spirit without a corresponding exercise of discipline on our part."[26] There is a righteousness in Christ that we

---

[25] Pettit, 271.

[26] Bridges, *The Discipline of Grace*, 132.

already possess (Rom. 3:21–26), but there is also a righteousness we pursue (Heb. 12:14).

Unfortunately, some Christians drift toward passivity in their approach to spiritual formation. They rightly believe that God is the one who transforms, but they wrongly assume zero responsibility for their maturation. Though transformation is primarily the work of the Holy Spirit, it very much requires our active pursuit. David Powlison emphasizes, "by definition, a person who changes takes action. You do something."[27] The Bible is full of commands that God expects us to obey through effort. For example, God commands us to:

- Put to death the works of the flesh. – Rom. 8:13
- Put off the old self and put on the new. – Eph. 4:22–24
- Put to death what is earthly in us – Col. 3:5
- Fight the good fight – 1 Tim. 6:12
- Strive to enter the narrow gate – Luke 13:24
- Run the race; discipline the body – 1 Cor. 9:24–27
- Press on; Strain forward – Phil. 3:12–14
- Make every effort – 2 Peter 1:5

We are responsible to obey these commands. Christians must actively pursue holiness because "holiness is not a condition into which we drift."[28] Jonathan Edwards said, "A true and faithful Christian does not make holy living an accidental thing. It is his great concern. As the business of the soldier is to fight, so the business of the Christian is to be like Christ." The primary way we fight for holiness is through the spiritual disciplines, which will be addressed in Chapter Five.

---

[27] Powlison, 69.
[28] Wilhoit, 39.

Sanctification Is a Joint Venture

God is sovereign over transformation, *and* humans have a responsibility in the process. Therefore, theologians describe spiritual formation as *synergistic*, a joint venture between God and man. As we consider "the whole counsel of God" (Acts 20:27), it is clear that what God has predestined for us, he has commanded us to pursue. There is no conflict between God's sovereign will, which he will accomplish, and his moral will for us, which we are to pursue. God will do his part in the transformation process, but we are responsible to do our part as well. We must avoid either-or extremes by realizing spiritual transformation is neither passivity nor performance but a partnership.

Spiritual formation is divine-human synergy over a lifetime.[29] Divine-human synergy is evident in both the Old and New Testaments. In the Old Testament, for example, God tells the Levites, "Keep my statutes and do them. I am the Lord, who sanctifies you" (Lev. 20:8). The Levites were responsible for obeying God's commands while knowing it was God who sanctified them. Psalm 127:1 says, "Unless the Lord builds the house, its builders labor in vain. Unless the Lord watches over the city, the watchmen stand guard in vain." The builders must work, and the watchmen must stand guard, but they must carry out their responsibilities in total dependence on God, or else they labor in vain.[30]

The New Testament describes divine-human synergy as believers working out our own salvation with fear and trembling while knowing it is God who works in us, both to will and to work for his good pleasure (Phil. 2:12–13). Divine-human synergy involves Christians "toiling and struggling" toward spiritual maturity while knowing we are only able to do so because of "his energy that he

---

[29] Eric Geiger, Michael Kelley, and Philip Nation, *Transformational Discipleship: How People Really Grow* (Nashville, TN: B&H Publishing, 2012), 57.

[30] Bridges, *The Discipline of Grace*, 131.

powerfully works in us" (Col. 1:29). The apostle Paul models divine-human synergy because he fully understands God's sovereignty, yet he works hard to fulfill his mission. Referring to his hard work, Paul says, "though it was not I, but the grace of God that is with me" (1 Cor. 15:10). Dallas Willard describes divine-human synergy when he says, "God's grace will accompany us every step of the way, but it will never permit us to be merely passive in our spiritual formation in Christ."[31]

The biblical writers consistently use agricultural metaphors to capture the interplay between humans and the divine in spiritual formation.[32] Consider the farming illustration the apostle Paul uses in 1 Corinthians 3:6–7. He says, "I planted, Apollos watered, but God gave the growth. So neither he who plants nor he who waters is anything, but only God who gives the growth." In the business of farming, there are certain things farmers must do, such as plow, plant, fertilize, irrigate, cultivate, and harvest. However, there are some things farmers cannot do, such as control the weather and make the crops grow. If a farmer neglects his responsibilities, he will not produce a crop. As in the case of farming, God has ordained certain disciplines or practices that are necessary for us to grow in holiness. Our responsibility is to cultivate godliness while depending on God to give growth. Just as an airplane must have both wings to fly, so we must exercise both discipline and dependence in our spiritual growth.[33]

Spiritual Growth Stoppers

As we pursue spiritual growth, invisible forces within the supernatural world will oppose us. These spiritual powers of darkness and wickedness seek to stop our spiritual growth (Eph. 6:12–13). At

---

[31] Andrews, 51.

[32] Wilhoit, 20.

[33] Bridges, *The Discipline of Grace*, 130.

the point of salvation, every Christian is enlisted as a soldier in the Lord's army (2 Tim. 2:3–4). Our fight is against the world, the flesh, and the devil. These enemies can be collectively referred to as the "trinity of evil."[34] Paul reveals the trinity of evil as he addresses the Ephesians: "And you were dead in the trespasses and sins in which you once walked, following the course of this *world*, following the *prince of the power of the air [devil]*, the spirit that is now at work in the sons of disobedience—among whom we all once lived in the passions of our *flesh*" (Eph. 2:1–3, emphasis mine). The world, the flesh, and the devil are not independent of one another; rather, they work together to destroy the Christian. The destructive system of the world, dominated by Satan, provides endless temptations to indulge the sinful flesh. As Christians, we never mature past these three enemies. Instead, as we grow, we become increasingly aware of and able to navigate conflicts with these enemies.[35]

The World

In one sense, the world is good; God made the world, loves the world, and is redeeming the world. Yet, in another sense, the world is bad; since the fall of man, the world is a place of sin, evil, suffering, destruction, and death. Describing the world as our enemy, Dr. John Koessler says, "the 'world' is both the realm of Satan and the domain of the flesh."[36] He adds, "Whenever we act in the flesh or in a way contrary to Christ's interests, we are being worldly. Christ… loves the world but He does not love worldliness."[37]

John describes the danger and wickedness of worldliness when he says, "Do not love the world or the things in the world. If anyone loves the world, the love of the Father is not in him. For all that is

---

[34] Andrews, 47.
[35] Howard, 188.
[36] Koessler, 187.
[37] Ibid., 187.

in the world—the desires of the flesh and the desires of the eyes and pride of life—is not from the Father but is from the world… the whole world lies in the power of the evil one" (1 Jn. 2:15–16; 5:19). Paul also cautions against conformity to worldliness (Rom. 12:2), which includes a love for temporal things like possessions, popularity, power, position, people-pleasing, and pride.[38]

May our legacy not be like Demas's, who walked away from Jesus because of his love for worldliness (2 Tim. 4:10). While the world fights for our attention and affection, God commands us to seek another world; his kingdom (Mt. 6:10). The church must represent God's kingdom of light amid a dark world; we must be *in* the world but not *of* the world (Jn. 17:15–18). Christians have dual citizenships; we are temporary citizens of the earth, but we are eternal citizens of God's kingdom.

The Flesh

Not only do we battle against the external influences of the world, but we also have an internal battle against the flesh. The flesh as our enemy refers not to our physical body but to that part of our nature that is bent on resisting God. The flesh represents our sinful nature, which all people are born into.[39] Prior to salvation, our sinful nature dominates us. In Christ, we are no longer slaves to sin but slaves to righteousness (Rom. 6:19). When Paul contrasts the flesh and the spirit in Galatians 5:16–18, he is contrasting the sinful nature with the renewed power the Holy Spirit gives us. Although sin no longer has control over us (Rom. 8), we still fight against the old sinful nature. Though the spirit is often willing, the flesh is weak.

The Corinthians are examples of those who allowed the flesh to hinder their spiritual growth. Paul tells them, "I, brothers, could not address you as spiritual people, but as people of the *flesh*, as infants

---

[38] Gallaty, 76.
[39] Koessler, 77.

in Christ. I fed you with milk, not solid food, for you were not ready for it. And even now you are not yet ready" (1 Cor. 3:1–2, emphasis mine). Paul was disappointed because the Corinthians allowed their fleshly desires to hinder their spiritual maturity. The role of the Christian is to put off the old self, which is corrupt through deceitful desires and put on the new self, created after the likeness of God in true righteousness and holiness (Eph. 4:22–24).[40] We must "put on the Lord Jesus Christ, and make no provision for the flesh, to gratify its desires" (Rom. 13:14).

The Devil

To disbelieve in Satan is to disbelieve scripture. Every book in the New Testament, along with seven Old Testament books, refers to Satan. He is called *the devil* (Mt. 4:1; 13:39; 25:41; Rev. 12:9; 20:2), *the serpent* (2 Cor. 11:3; Rev. 12:9; 20:2), *Beelzebub* (Mt. 10:25; 12:24,27; Lk. 11:15), *the ruler of this world* (Jn. 12:31; 14:30; 16:11), *the evil one* (Mt. 13:9; 1 Jn. 2:13), and *the dragon* (Rev. 12:9).[41] The devil is a real being who is prowling around like a lion seeking to steal, kill, and destroy (1 Pet. 5:8; Jn. 10:10). He is described in scripture as an adversary (Lk. 22:3), a slanderer (1 Pet. 5:8), a destroyer (Rev. 9:11), a tempter (Mt. 4:3), an accuser (Rev. 12:10), a deceiver (Rev. 12:9), a murderer (Jn. 8:44), and a liar (Jn. 8:44). Jesus names Satan as the origin of evil (Jn. 8:44). Unbelievers are described in scripture as being blinded by Satan and held captive to do his will (2 Cor. 4:3–4; 2 Tim. 2:26). They are described as being under his dominion and subjects of his kingdom (Acts 26:18;

---

[40] A helpful exercise for all Christians is to go through the lists of sins of the flesh and identify areas of personal temptation. These lists can be found in 1 Corinthians 6:9–10, Galatians 5:19–21, Ephesians 4:25–31, and Colossians 3:5,8–9. These are not exhaustive lists, but they help us identify common sins.
[41] Gallaty, 81.

Col. 1:13). J.I. Packer accurately expresses how Christians should understand Satan:

> He should be taken seriously, for malice and cunning make him fearsome; yet not so seriously as to provoke abject terror of him, for he is a beaten enemy. Satan is stronger than we are, but Christ has triumphed over Satan (Matt. 12:29), and Christians will triumph over him too if they resist him with the resources that Christ supplies (Eph. 6:10 13; James 4:7; 1 Pet. 5:9–10).[42]

Although Satan has ultimately been defeated by Christ, our war with him is not over. The devil and his demons will relentlessly try to prevent our spiritual formation by all means possible. Therefore, we should remain watchful, resistant to evil, and firm in our faith (1 Pet. 5:9). We should put on the armor of God in order to stand against the schemes of the devil (Eph. 6:10–11). In doing so, we must remember, "He who is in us is greater than he who is in the world" (1 Jn. 4:4). We are powerless to overcome the world, the flesh, and the devil on our own, but Jesus has overcome these enemies. In him, we have victory!

---

[42] J.I. Packer, *Concise Theology: A Guide to Historic Christian Beliefs* (Carol Stream, IL: Tyndale House, 1993), 70.

DISCUSSION QUESTIONS:

Is it possible to be justified without resulting life change? Explain.

What is spiritual formation?

What are some biblical words that are interchangeable with *spiritual formation*?

How would you explain the *already/not yet* paradox of the Christian faith?

Why is it helpful for a Christian to remember the butterfly?

When does our sanctification end?

What are the three primary means God uses to transform us?

Do we have a responsibility in the transformation process? Explain.

What does it mean that sanctification is *synergistic*?

What three primary enemies must we battle in our pursuit of holiness?

If our spiritual growth is hindered, what might be the cause?

Is holiness the primary pursuit of your life?

3
CHAPTER

Holistic Holiness: Head, Heart, and Hands

You shall love the Lord your God with all your heart and with
all your soul and with all your mind and with all your strength.
– Jesus in Mark 12:30

Scripture makes plain, the Christian life is a multidimensional
reality…holistic Christian existence is irreducibly thinking,
loving, and doing––mind, heart, and hands.
– David Mathis[1]

Physical well-being requires proper exercise, a healthy diet,
adequate sleep, regular check-ups with a physician, necessary
treatment of injury and illness, and so on. If one component
of physical health is neglected, negatively impacted, or taken to
extremes, a person's entire well-being is affected. For example, parents
often experience sleep deprivation as a result of tending to newborn
babies throughout the night. Sleep deprivation negatively affects
energy levels required to exercise. The downward spiral continues
as lack of sleep and exercise cause the parent to be less energetic,

---

[1] John Piper and David Mathis, eds., *Thinking. Loving. Doing.: A Call to
Glorify God with Heart and Mind* (Wheaton, IL: Crossway, 2011), 15.

less mentally alert, and less concerned about eating properly. Sleep deprivation causes a domino effect as it impacts other areas of a parent's well-being. The same domino effect will take place if a person chooses to sleep too much, or eat an unhealthy diet, or ignore symptoms of illness, etc. Spiritual well-being is like physical well-being. If we neglect or take to extremes any component, our overall spiritual formation will be negatively affected.

So far in this book, we have established that genuine salvation always results in transformation into the image of Christ. In this chapter, we will highlight spiritual formation as *holistic*, meaning there are interconnected parts that make up the whole, and each part affects the others. In this holistic approach, the whole is greater than the sum of the parts, and the parts are increasingly related to the whole.[2] Because sin has penetrated our head, heart, and hands, there is no part of our being that doesn't need transformation. God intends for newborn Christians to gradually become like Jesus in *every* way (Lk. 6:40). Therefore, holistic spiritual formation stresses the centrality of Christ over every component of our lives (head, heart, and hands). If we neglect to approach spiritual formation holistically, we will stagger our growth and likely end up in a pit. Unless providentially prevented or hindered, spiritual formation should be holistic.

The Greatest Commandment

When asked by a scribe what the greatest commandment is, Jesus replies, "The most important is, 'Hear, O Israel: The Lord our God, the Lord is one. And you shall love the Lord your God with all your heart and with all your soul and with all your mind and with all your strength.' The second is this: 'You shall love your neighbor as yourself.' There is no other commandment greater than these" (Mk.

---

[2] Kenneth Boa, *Conformed to His Image* (Grand Rapids, MI: Zondervan, 2001), 202.

12:29–31). Jesus loves God and others in precisely this way, and he calls his followers to do the same. The Great Commandment, which has been called the North Star of spiritual formation, is the greatest aim of the Christian life.[3] As we love God and love people, we are transformed, becoming what God created us to be. If the greatest command is to love God with all that we are, the greatest sin is not to do so.

Pastor and author Greg Ogden notes, "we were made from love and for love. Just as God unconditionally committed himself to us, so we in turn are to unreservedly devote all our faculties toward finding our fulfillment in God."[4] Regarding our human faculties, to love God with all our heart, soul, mind, and strength is to love him with *all* that we are. However, we must not overlook the fact that Jesus mentioned the faculties separately, indicating that loving God can be broken down into fundamental components.

The broad semantic range of the words heart, soul, mind, and strength overlaps considerably. These terms are sometimes used interchangeably and can mean different things in different contexts, causing interpreters anguish and confusion at times. So, for the purposes of this book, we will take a practical and straightforward approach to the human faculties. We will consider spiritual formation in terms of *head, heart,* and *hands.*[5] As we do so, we will maintain biblical integrity while avoiding unnecessary confusion and complexity.

---

[3] James Wilhoit, *Spiritual Formation as if the Church Mattered: Growing in Christ Through Community* (Grand Rapids, MI: Baker Academic, 2008), 45.

[4] Greg Ogden, *The Essential Commandment: A Disciple's Guide to Loving God and Others* (Downers Grove, IL: InterVarsity Press, 2011), 29.

[5] In the *head, heart, and hands* paradigm, the *soul* can be represented by a combination of the *head* and *heart.*

Head, Heart, and Hands: Defined

Head

As we define the *head*,[6] we must acknowledge that the *head* and the *heart* are intimately connected in scripture. For example, Matthew 9:4 records Jesus's reaction to the scribes after he heals and forgives a person with paralysis: "Jesus, knowing their *thoughts*, said, 'Why do you *think* evil in your *hearts*?'" (emphasis mine) Jesus views the minds and hearts of the scribes as being closely connected. Not only are the mind and heart closely associated throughout scripture, but sometimes they are used interchangeably in reference to the core of a human being. Nevertheless, the mind and heart are also referred to separately on many occasions, such as the Great Commandment; so, we know the mind and heart are not identical.[7] For the purposes of this book, we will address the head and the heart separately. We will operate with the following definition: the *head* represents one's thought life.

Heart

The word *heart* occurs over five hundred times in the Bible and most often signifies one's inner self, or core. Therefore, we will operate with the following definition: the *heart* represents one's inner self. The inner self, or core of a person, is multifaceted. As a result, the word *heart* in the Bible can represent different facets of one's inner being at different times, depending on the context. The facets of the *heart* include one's affections (what we love), will (what we choose), character (who we are), and emotions (how we feel).

---

[6] I will use *head* and *mind* interchangeably throughout this book.
[7] John Piper, *Think: The Life of the Mind and the Love of God* (Wheaton, IL: Crossway, 2010), 84.

Hands

Jesus commands his followers to love God with all their strength. Therefore, spiritual formation certainly involves action, or doing. For the purposes of this book, we will operate with the following definition: the *hands* represent one's actions. More specifically, the *hands* represent one's active obedience to God and good works toward others. God does not save his people simply to think rightly and feel rightly, but "for good works, which God prepared beforehand, that we should walk in them" (Eph. 2:10). James reminds Christians to be "doers of the word, and not hearers only" (Js. 1:22) because faith without works is dead (Js. 2:17). Action is indispensable to genuine Christian faith.

Head, Heart, and Hands: Interconnected

The Great Commandment is fulfilled not just through the head, the heart, or the hands, but through all three working together simultaneously. Thus, Christian formation is like a three-legged stool; each leg, represented by either the head, heart, or hands, is necessary for the stool to stand. God's Word consistently brings together the head, heart, and hands. In addition to the Great Commandment, here are other examples of this interconnectedness:

- "For Ezra set his heart *[heart]* to study *[head]* the Law of the Lord, and to do it *[hands]* and to teach his statutes and rules in Israel." – Ezr. 7:10
- "Give me understanding, *[head]* that I may keep your law *[hands]* and observe it with all my heart." *[heart]* – Ps. 119:34
- "Desire *[heart]* without knowledge *[head]* is not good, and whoever makes haste with his feet *[hands]* misses his way." – Prov. 19:2

- "Now when they heard this *[head]* they were cut to the heart, *[heart]* and said to Peter and the rest of the apostles, 'Brothers, what shall we do?'" *[hands]* – the response to Peter's sermon at Pentecost in Acts 2:37
- "Make every effort to supplement your faith with virtue, *[heart]* and virtue with knowledge, *[head]* and knowledge with self-control, *[hands]* and self-control with steadfastness, and steadfastness with godliness, ..." – 2 Pet. 1:5–6

Like Ezra, our goal as we read scripture should be to know it, implant it within the heart, and apply it to life. These head-heart-hands connections are often difficult. But, if the connections are not made, transformation will be thwarted.

The interconnectedness of the head, heart, and hands was perceived and described by Christians throughout the ages. Here are some examples from recent decades:

- *D. Martin Lloyd-Jones* explains the interconnection as follows: "The heart is always to be influenced through the understanding—the mind, then the heart, then the will... But God forbid that anyone should think that it ends with the intellect. It starts there, but it goes on. It then moves the heart and finally the man yields his will...The Christian life is a glorious perfect life that takes up and captivates the entire personality."[8]
- *Evan Howard* describes the interconnection as a complex dance in which "the enlightenment of our intellect triggers a new sense of beauty. This tugs at our emotions. Transformed emotions motivate our will, and actions follow. New action

---

[8] D. Martyn Lloyd-Jones, *Spiritual Depression: Its Causes and Cure* (Grand Rapids, MI: Eerdmans, 1965), 61–62.

leads to new experiences, which in turn inform our thinking and feeling. And on and on it goes."[9]

- *David Mathis* states, "Scripture makes plain, the Christian life is a multidimensional reality...holistic Christian existence is irreducibly thinking, loving, and doing—mind, heart, and hands."[10]

- *John Piper* addresses the interconnection when he says, "the fires of love *[heart]* for God drive the engines of thought *[head]* and deed *[hands]*...Thinking feeds the fire, and the fire fuels more thinking and doing."[11]

- *Dennis Hollinger* summarizes the interconnectedness of the head, heart, and hands as follows: "Theology, spirituality, and Christian practice can never be separated. Our beliefs, inner sentiments and actions are all part of each other. We will have a greater chance of getting our theology right if our affections and actions are in accordance with the truth of the living God and God's revealed patterns. We will have a greater chance of being drawn closer to the intimate presence and power of God if our thinking and practices accord with God's designs. And we will have a greater chance of getting our actions and practices right when our minds and hearts are rooted in and captured by the reality of the living, triune God."[12]

A separation of head, heart, and hands is inconsistent with God's design for believers. When they join in harmony together, we

---

[9] Evan Howard, *A Guide to Christian Spiritual Formation: How Scripture, Spirit, Community, and Mission Shape Our Souls* (Grand Rapids, MI: Baker Academic, 2018), 177.

[10] Piper and Mathis, eds., 15.

[11] Piper, 89.

[12] Dennis P. Hollinger, *Head, Heart & Hands: Bringing Together Christian Thought, Passion and Action* (Downers Grove, IL: InterVarsity Press, 2005),187.

recognize that the head, heart, and hands are not three distinct parts, but three interacting dimensions of our whole being.[13]

There is a necessary tension between the head, heart, and hands. John Piper acknowledges this tension when he states, "Thinking and feeling and doing jostle each other in my life, jockeying for more room...Should I be doing more, thinking more, feeling more, expressing more feeling?"[14] Exactly how the head, heart, and hands join together, feed, and sustain one another remains mysterious, but the fact remains that genuine transformation requires Christians to *know* and *be* and *do*, all to the glory of God.

Lopsided Formation

Too often, individuals, churches, even entire denominations practice a lopsided faith. All of us are shaped by culture, giftedness, church background, and personality. These things tend to predispose us to a faith of the head, heart, or hands. Many Christian traditions, though well-intentioned, emphasize one or two of these components at the expense of others, unintentionally giving Christians a distorted view of spiritual formation. Some traditions are prone to a faith of the head because they elevate correct doctrine and theology. Other traditions are prone to a faith of the heart because they emphasize emotional experiences. Still, other traditions are prone to a faith of the hands because they accentuate practical Christian living. Correct doctrine, meaningful worship experiences, and practical Christian living are all good and necessary aspects of Christianity. However, taken alone, each represents a fragmented faith with imbalances and inadequacies.[15]

---

[13] Hollinger, 32.
[14] Piper, 28.
[15] Hollinger, 32.

Pitfalls of the Head, Heart, and Hands

As we journey along the path of spiritual formation, we must avoid the pitfalls. If we neglect or take to extremes the head, heart, or hands, we may end up in a pit. In identifying pitfalls of the head, heart, and hands, we will lean on the expertise of Dr. Dennis Hollinger in his book *Head, Heart, and Hands: Bringing Together Christian Thought, Passion, and Action.*

Head-only Faith

What happens when a Christian aims to love God with all his mind while neglecting the heart and hands? What happens when the mind is taken to unhealthy extremes? Consider this case study:

> Meet Jeff. Jeff was a thoughtful Christian. He grew up in a secular home that had no time for matters of religion, but during his high school years he came to faith in Christ. Because family and friends chided him for his newfound beliefs and commitment, Jeff began to seek answers for the hard questions he faced.
>
> By the time Jeff graduated from a university as a philosophy major, he had developed intellectual rigor regarding Christian beliefs and apologetics. He knew the difficult and skeptical questions to his faith, but read broadly to find answers to the challenges. Jeff often found himself in the middle of intellectual debates with fellow students and had ready answers for them. Christians on campus frequently found help through his philosophical and theological responses to the tough issues. Jeff knew what he believed and why he believed it.

But, interestingly, there were significant elements of true and vital faith that seemed to be missing in Jeff's life. Personal prayer, spiritual disciplines and fellowship with other Christians increasingly became a low priority in his life. At times they were hardly evident. In fact, he sometimes showed contempt for the personal piety of other believers, noting their shallow emotionality and lack of theological or philosophical depth. Moreover, in his zeal to defend the faith against skeptics, he sometimes showed a lack of compassion and care for people.[16]

Jeff has what can be considered a "faith of the head." Jeff, like many Christians, understands his faith to be primarily an intellectual endeavor. For Jeff, Christianity is mainly a set of beliefs that he is supposed to follow. Therefore, Jeff's spiritual growth is primarily about knowledge and thinking.

Hollinger observes three major consequences when the head is supreme, and the other dimensions of faith are neglected:[17]

1. *Cold, dead orthodoxy*: Head-only faith leads to cold, dead religion. Lifeless intellectualism fails to give attention to human character and actions. Head-only faith causes one's relationship with God to lack vitality and reality.
2. *Self-deception*: Head-only faith leads to self-deception in how people perceive themselves and God. People with this sort of faith tend to believe that once they have articulated and defended the truth, their Christian obligation has been performed.

---

[16] Hollinger, 13–14.
[17] Ibid., 63–66.

3. *Abandonment of faith*: Head-only faith can lead a person to abandon the faith, indicating the person was not truly saved to begin with.

Approaching transformation as merely Bible knowledge devalues spiritual growth and denies the power of the gospel. The mind alone cannot sustain a genuine faith. We must not confuse Bible knowledge with spiritual maturity. Just because a person knows the Bible does not mean he or she is being transformed by it. When transformation occurs, there is an increasing hunger for more knowledge of Jesus and his Word, but the primary focus of acquiring knowledge must be the ongoing renewal of the heart.[18]

The Neglected Mind

Let's consider the other extreme; what happens when the mind is missing or minimized in our spiritual formation? What happens when we neglect the mind? Let's consider another case study:

> Meet Christina. Christina read the Bible, emphasizing that it was not for knowledge and understanding but for a "spiritual zap," as she termed it. She yearned for the Word to move her heart and she yearned to feel the presence and power of God. When it came to making decisions in life, she relied little on the wisdom of others or on reflection of the situation at hand; she prayed for God's direct, inner direction. She felt the leading of God. The Lord was her personal friend.

---

[18] Eric Geiger, Michael Kelley, and Philip Nation, *Transformational Discipleship: How People Really Grow* (Nashville, TN: B&H Publishing Group, 2012), 28.

But there were aspects of Christina's life that caused some to wonder. At one point, she had a very emotional, mystical experience in which she claimed that God was telling her to divorce her husband. When friends in her church raised questions from a biblical standpoint, she responded, "I know what the Bible says, but this is what God has told me to do, and I'm going to do it." God had spoken deeply to her soul, so she said, and the divorce became reality.[19]

Christina has what we might call a "faith of the heart." Her faith is seemingly alive and vibrant at the heart level, but very dangerous at the mind level.

Hollinger reveals three significant consequences when the mind is neglected in one's spiritual formation:[20]

1. *Incomplete faith*: Like Christina, Christians who neglect the mind usually resort to a faith dominated by feelings and become spiritually dependent on their emotional state or on a series of peak "spiritual experiences," which they seek to continually replicate. Whenever the mind is denigrated, emotions and personal preferences will be given priority over truth.

2. *Unorthodox faith*: Neglecting the mind leads to a deviant faith. Christianity that neglects the mind breeds beliefs and practices that are incongruent with the Bible and a Christian worldview.

3. *Inability to engage the world*: When the head is neglected, Christians will not be able to discern elements that are compatible with the Christian faith, those that are clearly incompatible, and those that are somewhere in between.

---

[19] Hollinger, 14.
[20] Ibid., 58–62.

Thus, Christians will lose the ability to be the salt and light of the world that God intends.

Christ calls us to love God with all our minds. Therefore, to neglect the mind causes an incomplete, abnormal, and unfruitful faith. Without the mind, genuine faith cannot and will not be sustained. In some cases, the neglect of the mind may indicate an illegitimate faith.

Heart-only Faith

What happens when a follower of Jesus aims to love God with all his heart while neglecting the head and hands? What happens when the heart is taken to unhealthy extremes? Recall Christina's heart-only faith; though the heart is essential in spiritual growth, it should never operate apart from thought and action. Often, broken emotional experiences must be subjected to the truth. After all, the heart can be very deceitful (Jer. 17:9).

Hollinger identifies three major consequences when the heart is supreme, and the other dimensions of faith are neglected: [21]

1. *Vulnerable to inward states*: When our hearts dominate us, we easily allow our internal state to define our faith. God will only be real when we feel him.
2. *Inadequate resources for engaging the world*: Heart-only faith typically lacks the depth, clarity, theological understanding, and biblical wisdom necessary to engage the world with the biblical gospel.
3. *Heterodoxy*: Heart-only faith leads to deviant faith. Heart-only faith tends to abandon biblical, theological, and historical understandings of the Christian faith in favor of more immediate feelings of the heart. Hollinger

---

[21] Hollinger, 99–103

notes, "Revivalism, when focused primarily on emotional experience without the guidance of the Bible, theology and the wisdom of the larger church, has the potential to be heart religion run amuck."[22]

If we focus primarily on the heart in our spiritual formation, we will become spiritually vulnerable and ineffective in representing Christ to the world. Many who ignore the head and hands at the expense of the heart eventually stray from the faith once for all delivered to the saints (Jude 1:3), revealing an illegitimate faith.

The Neglected Heart

Let's consider the other extreme; what happens when the heart is missing or minimized in our spiritual formation? What happens when we neglect the heart? Let's consider another case study:

> Meet Jennifer. Jennifer grew up in a home and congregation that prized solid biblical teaching and the practice of personal piety. She went to church several times a week and was soaked in an "indoctrination" of the faith.
> When Jennifer went off to college, she was exposed to new ways of thinking and began to react to her own family and church. She didn't reject her faith, but believed it needed a radically different form. For Jennifer, action was what it was all about. She came to believe that most acts of piety were hypocritical forms of religiosity that Jesus had repudiated in His injunctions against the Pharisees. The point was not primarily to understand the faith, and certainly not to feel it emotionally. The whole

---

[22] Hollinger, 104.

point of following Jesus was to do it…embody His teachings and actions.

Acts of justice and compassion were the focus of Jennifer's Christianity. She became involved in various programs and movements of social justice in her community, attempting to address issues of environment, race, and poverty. Jennifer wanted to be the hands and feet of Jesus.

But, interestingly, there were some missing parts to Jennifer's faith. She confessed to a friend she did little to nurture her spirituality. She had minimal time for her local church and most of her reading focused on social issues. As she put it, "I just don't find theology to be helpful to the causes." [23]

Jennifer has what we might call a "faith of the hands." Jennifer represents a distorted faith of action that mostly lacks head and heart involvement.

Hollinger explains four major consequences when the heart is missing or minimized in one's faith:[24]

1. *Loss of divine presence and power*: A heartless faith will cause God to become an idea or concept instead of a personal being who provides comfort, joy, peace, forgiveness, and power.

2. *Loss of mystery*: Christianity is a faith that involves, even requires, mystery. Dr. Hollinger states, "Vital spirituality needs a sense of mystery to grow deeper in Christ…Only in allowing for mystery is profound worship and living trust truly possible. And only with attentiveness to the heart do we encounter such mystery."[25] Mystery causes necessary

---

[23] Hollinger, 15.

[24] Ibid., 92–98.

[25] Ibid., 95.

humility and dependence on God. Mystery grows with knowledge of God.

3. *Loss of character—replaced with legalism*: When the heart is neglected, moral character will deteriorate. When moral character deteriorates, there is a tendency to turn to legalism to address one's moral decline.

4. *Loss of true understanding*: Hollinger says, "When our heart is not attuned to God, we can be sure that it will negatively impact our understanding of God and His ways (theology) and of God's designs for daily living (ethics)."[26]

The heart is mandatory in our spiritual growth because without it, spirituality becomes a set of beliefs or a course of action. Because the Pharisees of Jesus's day were legalistic and lacked heart, Jesus called them "whitewashed tombs" who "appear beautiful" on the outside "but within are full of dead people's bones and all uncleanness" (Mt. 23:27). The heart is required for a person to truly know God. A heartless faith could prove to be a Christ-less faith.

Hands-only Faith

What happens when a follower of Jesus aims to love God with all his strength yet neglects the head and heart? What happens when we take the hands to unhealthy extremes? Recall Jennifer's hands-only faith; she was very active, but she was not guided by or grounded in God's Word. She was not motivated and sustained by a heart focused on the presence and power of Christ in her life. As Jennifer saw it, the Christian faith was primarily about the hands—actions of justice and mercy.[27] Jennifer represents a distorted faith of action that mostly lacks head and heart involvement. Unfortunately, religious

---

[26] Hollinger, 97.
[27] Ibid., 129.

zeal—no matter how vigorous and pious—is worthless if it's not grounded in the mind and heart of Christ.

Hollinger identifies four substantial consequences of a hands-only faith that neglects the head and the heart:[28]

1. *Self-sufficiency (works righteousness)*: When one is engaged in the world without divine guidance and empowerment, he or she naturally looks within for the guidance that should come from God. Inward focus reveals human pride, and can even become a form of works-righteousness.

2. *Superficial faith*: Action without theology breeds a shallow faith that often lacks the ability to weather the intellectual, cultural, and personal storms of life.

3. *Heterodox faith:* Hands-only faith leads to an abnormal faith as it causes theological understandings and practices that are contrary to scripture and the historic Christian faith.

4. *Misuses of proclamation*: Hands-only faith leads to hazardous evangelism. Commitment to the truth of the gospel and Christlike character must always accompany effective evangelism. Unfortunately, hands-only faith proponents tend to adhere to and promote a works-based gospel of legalism.

Action is irreplaceable in the Christian faith, but it's dangerous when action becomes the defining aspect of one's faith. Works of justice and mercy detached from theology and a heart for God lead to a distorted faith. Worst case scenario, a faith of the hands may expose conversion to the false gospel of works righteousness.

---

[28] Hollinger, 134–139.

The Neglected Hands

Let's consider the other extreme; what happens when the hands are missing or minimized in our spiritual formation? What happens when we neglect the hands? Recall Jeff, the thoughtful Christian who had a ready answer for the questions about his faith. Jeff knew the Bible, theology, and apologetics better than most of his peers. But as Jeff lived his faith, it was almost entirely through the mind. Jeff's approach to Christianity was distorted in two ways. First of all, he perceived witnessing to be primarily about winning rational arguments. Many who listened to him did not experience the love of Christ. Secondly, Jeff had a minimal emphasis on action.[29]

Hollinger identifies three main consequences when action is neglected or minimized in one's pursuit of holiness:[30]

1. *A dead faith*: James made it abundantly clear that faith without action is dead faith (Js. 2:14–17). So, if a person claims proper belief and proper feeling but consistently neglects action, this is a good reason for this person to question the legitimacy of his or her faith.
2. *Impact on our thinking*: Neglecting the hands distorts thinking. Because of the interconnection, proper action edifies proper thinking while disobedience distorts right thinking.
3. *Impact on the sentiments of our heart*: Neglecting the hands distorts the heart. Once again, because of the interconnection, our heart is affected by our actions. When proper action is missing, our hearts will grow cold and fall short of God's intentions.

---

[29] Hollinger, 128.
[30] Ibid., 129–134.

Genuine faith always expresses itself through action. God creates us for good works, that we should walk in them (Eph. 2:10). In expressing our faith through action, we confirm a legitimate faith.

In summary, genuine transformation must be balanced and holistic, or else spiritual growth is hindered. A distorted faith of the head, heart, or hands both weakens the spiritual formation of Christians and exposes the illegitimate faith of false converts. Can you think of other pitfalls of the head, heart, or hands? Can you relate to Jeff, Christina, or Jennifer? Is your spiritual formation lopsided? Are you prone to a faith of the head, heart, or hands? Did any of these pitfalls resonate with you?

Diagnostic Test

I'd like to close this chapter with a simple diagnostic test to determine your spiritual growth tendencies and susceptibilities. Consider the type of sermon you prefer. If given a choice, would you rather:

A. Listen to a sermon that targets your head; one that's heavy on doctrine and theology; one that challenges your intellect?
B. Listen to a sermon that targets your heart; one that's heavy on stories and illustrations that take you on an emotional roller coaster ride?
C. Listen to a sermon that targets your hands; one that's heavy on practical application; one that minimizes doctrine and illustrations and instead offers you a to-do list?

These are exaggerated options. Realistically, a good sermon targets the head, heart, and hands. But, if you can answer that question, it may help you understand more about your spiritual growth tendencies and susceptibilities. The point of this diagnostic test is to help you realize areas you might be weaker in so that you can address them and prevent lopsided spiritual growth.

The following chapters will help you understand exactly how you can strengthen your area(s) of weakness by pursuing the mind, heart, and hands of Christ.

I pray, "the God of peace himself [will] sanctify you *completely*, and may your whole spirit and soul and body be kept blameless at the coming of our Lord Jesus Christ. He who calls you is faithful; he will surely do it" (1 Thess. 5:23–24, emphasis mine). I pray, "the peace of God, which surpasses all understanding, will guard your *hearts* and your *minds* in Christ Jesus" (Phil. 4:7, emphasis mine).

DISCUSSION QUESTIONS:

How is spiritual formation like physical well-being?

What does it mean that spiritual formation is *holistic*?

How is the Great Commandment (Mk. 12:29–31) related to spiritual formation?

How does the author define the *head*, *heart*, and *hands*?

Can you describe the interrelation of the head, heart, and hands?

Do you agree that many individuals, churches, and denominations practice a "lopsided" faith? Why, or why not?

How has your culture, giftedness, church background, and personality shaped your spiritual formation?

Are you susceptible to any "pitfalls" of the head, heart, or hands? Explain.

What will you do to prevent imbalanced spiritual growth?

4
CHAPTER

Head: Pursuing the Mind of Christ

Do not be conformed to this world, but be transformed by the
renewal of your mind, that by testing you may discern what
is the will of God, what is good and acceptable and perfect.
– Romans 12:2

The renewal of the Christian mind is imperative...A
recovery of the life of the mind is essential for
the survival and well-being of the church.
– Alister McGrath[1]

Spiritual formation occurs, in part, through the transformation
of the mind. We cannot adequately reflect the heart of Christ
or the hands of Christ if we neglect the mind of Christ. Jesus
commands his followers, "You shall love the Lord your God with
all your... mind" (Mt. 22:37). To love God with all your mind is
to pursue the mind of Christ. The importance of the mind in the
Christian life cannot be overstated. The mind is essential to Christian
conversion, maturity, worship, faith, guidance, evangelism, and

---

[1] Alister McGrath, *Mere Discipleship: Growing in Wisdom and Hope* (Grand
Rapids, MI: Baker Books, 2018), 5–7.

ministry.[2] Our minds represent the means to Christlikeness, or the opposite, depending on how we use them. In Romans 12:2, Paul says our minds must be renewed if we are to live life to the full. Transformation of the mind enables us to escape the sinful patterns of the world in favor of knowing and doing God's perfect will.

Given the importance of the mind, it's no wonder Christianity is the greatest intellectual movement in history. Christians invented universities like Harvard, Yale, Oxford, and Cambridge out of a desire to glorify God with the mind. Unfortunately, it seems many Evangelical Christians today neglect their minds. In 1995, Mark Noll published an award-winning book called *The Scandal of the Evangelical Mind*. Noll's surprising conclusion after painstakingly examining the evangelical tradition was: "the scandal of the evangelical mind is that there is not much of an evangelical mind."[3] Dr. Al Mohler, president of Southern Baptist Theological Seminary, recently echoed Noll's findings by stating, "An essential dimension of Christian discipleship is the life of the mind, and this may well be the most neglected Christian responsibility of our times."[4] Neglecting the mind is no trivial matter because doing so dishonors God and hinders our spiritual formation. Furthermore, neglecting the mind makes one vulnerable and helpless, like a boat being tossed along the waves and carried by the winds of the sea (Eph. 4:14). If Noll and Mohler are right, Evangelicals have much room for improvement in the way we love God with our minds. Every Christian can and should pursue the mind of Christ.

In Chapter Three, we defined the *head/mind* to represent one's thought life. Therefore, to pursue the mind of Christ is to pursue Jesus's thought life (2 Pet. 3:18; Phil. 2:5). Jesus, as the

---

[2] Greg Ogden, *The Essential Commandment: A Disciple's Guide to Loving God and Others* (Downers Grove, IL: InterVarsity Press, 2011), 89.

[3] Mark Noll, *The Scandal of the Evangelical Mind* (Grand Rapids: MI: Eerdmans, 1994), 3.

[4] John Piper, *Think: The Life of the Mind and the Love of God* (Wheaton, IL: Crossway, 2010), 1.

ideal human, has a perfect mind. He alone flawlessly fulfilled the Great Commandment by loving the Father with all of his mind. Consequently, Jesus is our standard, and there is no other. As we follow Jesus, we shouldn't simply ask, "What would Jesus do?"; we must also consider, "How would Jesus think?" in any given situation. Spiritual formation is about progressively replacing sinful thoughts with the very thoughts that filled the mind of Jesus.

Fundamental Realities of the Mind

Before we discover how to pursue the mind of Christ, let's first consider three fundamental realities of the mind: (1) The mind shapes one's overall being; (2) The mind of Christ is accessible, but not fully realized; (3) A person cannot develop a Christian mind without help. These realities will aid us as we explore the pursuit of Christ's mind.

The Mind Shapes One's Overall Being

The mind is perhaps the most critical human faculty because it's through the mind that we see life. Jesus says in Matthew 6:22–23, "The eye is the lamp of the body. So, if your eye is healthy, your whole body will be full of light, but if your eye is bad, your whole body will be full of darkness. If then the light in you is darkness, how great is the darkness!" The "eye" in Jesus's statement represents one's mind, or center of thought. The way we think creates our attitudes, shapes our emotions, and governs our behavior; everything about us flows out of the way we think.[5]

---

[5] John Ortberg, *If You Want to Walk on Water, You've Got to Get Out of the Boat* (Grand Rapids, MI: Zondervan, 2001), 162.

The Mind of Christ Is Accessible but Not Fully Realized

Paul confidently tells the Corinthians at the beginning of his letter, "we have the mind of Christ" (1 Cor. 2:16). You may be wondering, if Christians already have the mind of Christ, what's the purpose of this chapter? Well, not so fast. Paul urges the Corinthians near the end of his letter, "Do not be children in your thinking" (1 Cor. 14:20). In a different context, Paul commands the Philippian believers to "Have the mind [of Christ]" (Phil. 2:5). How can Paul declare that Christians have the mind of Christ, and at the same time, command them not to think like children? Do Christians have the mind of Christ or not?

Upon conversion, every Christian receives free access to the mind of Christ. However, sin causes our minds to become overloaded, distracted, confused, stressed, undisciplined, and passive. As a result, we often fail to access the mind of Christ. So, the mind of Christ is available to us but not fully realized because of sin. Spiritual formation requires us to fight sin and brokenness and pursue the mind of Christ.

A Person Cannot Develop a Christian Mind Without Help

We are not alone in our pursuit of Christ's mind. We have a Helper. Spiritual formation as a joint venture between God and man is evident in the formation of our minds. Paul's instruction to Timothy is clear evidence of this joint venture; he tells Timothy, "Think over what I say, for the Lord will give you understanding in everything" (2 Tim. 2:7). Timothy was responsible for thinking, while it was the Lord who gave him understanding. The Lord, through the Holy Spirit, helps us take on the mind of Christ. The same Spirit who searches the depths of God dwells within Christians (1 Cor. 2:10). Professor Diane Chandler confirms, "When the Spirit of God resides within us, we have access to the mind of God. Only the Spirit, who knows the mind of God, can help us have the mind of Christ (1 Cor. 2:16)."[6] Although the Spirit helps us, he will not do the work of thinking for us. As we trust the Spirit, we are not freed from the responsibility to think. There is no shortcut to the knowledge of God. So, the question before us is not *if* we must pursue the mind of Christ; it's *how* we can pursue the mind of Christ.

Pursuing Jesus's Thought Life

We pursue the mind of Christ by pursuing his thought life. In order to act like Jesus and be like Jesus, we must think like Jesus. God creates humanity with the unique capacity to think, which gives us the moral obligation to use our minds to honor him. Dallas Willard says, "The ultimate freedom we have as human beings is the power to select what we will allow our minds to dwell upon..."[7] In other words, we are not victims of our thoughts. The realm of thought includes ideas, images, information, predispositions, expectations, memories, perceptions, and beliefs.

To think like Jesus may sound like a mystical, or even impossible, endeavor, but it's not. Jesus's thought patterns are on open display throughout scripture, and God commands us to pursue those thought patterns. Paul, in arguably the most popular verse regarding Christlike thought, commands the Philippians: "whatever is true, whatever is honorable, whatever is just, whatever is pure, whatever is lovely, whatever is commendable, if there is any excellence, if there is anything worthy of praise, *think* about these things" (Phil. 4:8, emphasis mine). In addition to Philippians 4:8, God also commands us to think like Jesus by:

---

[6] Diane Chandler, *Christian Spiritual Formation: An Integrated Approach for Personal and Relational Wholeness* (Downers Grove, IL: InterVarsity Press, 2014), 147.

[7] Dallas Willard, *Renewing the Christian Mind: Essays, Interviews, and Talks* (New York, NY: HarperCollins Publishers, 2016), 3.

- Setting the mind on the things of God (Mt. 16:23; Mk. 8:33)
- Setting the mind on the Spirit (Rom. 8:6)
- Focusing on eternity (2 Cor. 4:16–18; Col. 3:2)
- Renewing the mind (Eph. 4:22–24)
- Taking thoughts captive (2 Cor. 10:5)
- Being sober-minded (1 Pet. 1:13)
- Guarding the mind (Phil. 4:6–9)
- Avoiding double-mindedness (Js. 1:6–8)
- Maintaining a humble mind (Phil. 2:3)
- Sustaining a pure mind (Titus 1:15)
- Conserving a responsive mind (Lk. 24:45)
- Preserving a content mind (Phil. 4:12–13)
- Keeping an assured mind (1 Jn. 5:13)

The commands listed above are only a sampling of God's commandments regarding Christian thought. As we obey these commands, we think like Jesus.

In pursuing Jesus's thought life, we must remember that our minds will think about what we expose them to. The places we go, the content we read, the music we listen to, the images we see, the conversations we have, all shape our minds. Therefore, we must continually return to Philippians 4:8 and set our minds on what is true, honorable, pure, lovely, commendable, excellent, and praiseworthy. Greg Ogden describes spiritual formation as "a lifelong process of transformation in which we're continuously adjusting our thinking by banishing distortions of God's reality while putting on His new way of seeing."[8] Right thinking, by God's grace, leads to Christlikeness and greater fellowship with God.

---

[8] Ogden, 105.

Pursuing Truth

In our pursuit of Jesus's thought life, there is nothing more important than seeking truth and reason. Bill Hull helpfully notes, "It's one thing to believe in Jesus. It's quite another to believe what Jesus believed. And the first can't be what it should be without the second."[9] Disciples of Christ must progressively believe what Jesus believes, and Jesus believes truth. Pursuing the mind of Christ isn't merely seeking knowledge, but knowledge *of the truth*. This distinction is necessary because not all so-called "knowledge" is true. *Truth* can be defined as "that which is consistent with the mind, will, character, glory, and being of God."[10] The truth represents the way things actually are.

Pursuing truth is inherent to Christianity because the Christian faith is inseparable from truth. Consider what scripture teaches about truth:

- God is the "God of truth" (Ps. 31:5; Is. 65:16)
- God's Word is truth (Ps. 119:160; Ps. 138:2; Jn. 17:17)
- The Lord Jesus Christ, God in human flesh, is "full of grace and truth" (Jn. 1:14; Jn. 1:17)
- Jesus is "the way, and the truth, and the life" (Jn. 14:6; Eph. 4:21)
- Satan is described as one who has no truth in him (Jn. 8:44)
- The Holy Spirit is the "Spirit of truth" (Jn. 14:17; Jn. 15:26; Jn. 16:13; 1 Jn. 5:6)
- By believing the truth of the gospel, people are set free from sin and death (Jn. 8:32)
- The Holy Spirit seals the salvation of those who embrace "the message of truth" (Eph. 1:13)

---

[9] Bill Hull, *The Complete Book of Discipleship: On Being and Making Followers of Christ* (Colorado Springs, CO: NavPress, 2006), 130.

[10] John MacArthur, *The Truth War: Fighting For Certainty in an Age of Deception* (Nashville, TN: Thomas Nelson, 2007), 2.

- The church is the "pillar and support of the truth" (1 Tim. 3:15)
- The church is called to protect and proclaim the truth of the gospel (Col. 1:5)
- Spiritual warfare requires one to put on the belt of truth (Eph. 6:14)
- The only worship that is acceptable to God is worship in truth (Jn. 4:24)

To pursue the mind of Christ is to pursue truth. John Stott ventured to say that if we avoid the use of our minds to seek God's truth, we descend to the level of animals![11] The overwhelming message of scripture is that knowing the truth is crucial because we are transformed as we are informed.[12] God intends for us to know the truth so that the truth can set us free (Jn. 8:32).

Both Old and New Testaments contain exhortations to seek truth and store up knowledge. In the Old Testament, for example, the Proverbs command us to seek truth like people seek silver and gold (Prov. 2:4). Proverbs 15:14 says, "The heart of him who has understanding seeks knowledge, but the mouths of fools feed on folly." Again, Proverbs 18:15 says, "An intelligent heart acquires knowledge, and the ear of the wise seeks knowledge."

In the New Testament, Jesus, whose earthly ministry was centered on teaching the truth, invited his followers to a life of learning (Mt. 9:13; 11:29; 24:32). The Greek word for disciple, *mathetes*, actually means "learner" in its earliest usage.[13] Disciples are inherently people who learn; people who attain knowledge of the truth. Not only did Jesus elevate the need for knowledge during his

---

[11] John Stott, *Your Mind Matters: The Place of the Mind in the Christian Life* (Downers Grove, IL: InterVarsity Press, 2006), 31.

[12] Brian Hedges, *Christ Formed in You: The Power of the Gospel for Personal Change* (Wapwallopen, PN: Shepherd Press, 2010), 155.

[13] Preston Sprinkle, *Go: Returning Discipleship to the Frontlines of Faith* (Colorado Springs, CO: NavPress, 2016), 95.

earthly ministry, but so did his Apostles. For example, Peter writes, "make every effort to supplement your faith with virtue, and virtue with knowledge,…" (2 Pet. 1:5). Paul consistently prays for the churches he plants to grow in the knowledge of truth and wisdom (Eph. 1:17–19; 3:14–19; Phil. 1:9–11; Col. 1:9–10).

Pastor Max Anders states, "Whether we go to Scripture, experience, or common sense, we see that knowledge is a good thing, a powerful thing, and something that a Christian must commit himself to acquiring."[14] As we pursue truth, we find the answers to life's most important questions, such as: "Why am I here?"; "Is there a God?"; "If so, has he revealed himself to us?"; "How can I be right with God?"; and so on. As we attain truth, we are increasingly able to think like Jesus.

Truth is attained primarily through the Bible

All truth is God's truth, but God's Word is the primary vehicle of his self-revelation, his plan, and his purposes. We can learn about God to an extent through creation and conscience, or *general revelation* as theologians call it. Through general revelation, God makes his power, glory, and righteousness known to everyone so that the entire human race has no excuse to be ignorant of the truths of God (Rom. 1:19–20). While general revelation exposes all people to God, it's insufficient to provide answers to life's most important questions. Therefore, God reveals truth more specifically through Jesus and through the Bible, his written Word. Theologians call this *special revelation*. All proper learning should be through the lens of scripture. J.I. Packer notes the profound priority of the Bible in the transformation of the mind:

---

[14] Max Anders, *Brave New Discipleship: Cultivating Scripture-Driven Christians in a Culture-Driven World* (Nashville, TN: Thomas Nelson, 2015), 57.

> Man was made to know good with his mind, to desire it,…and to cleave to it…; the good in this case being God, his truth and his law. God accordingly moves us, not by direct action on the affections or will, but by addressing our mind with his word, and so bringing to bear on us the force of truth…Affection may be the helm of the ship, but the mind must steer; and the chart to steer is God's revealed truth.[15]

To know God is to know his Word, and to know his Word is to know the truth. Jesus was a profound student of God's written Word. So, to have the mind of Christ is to have a mind filled with scripture. From the foundation of knowing God through his Word, we are able to think fruitfully about all of life.[16] Diane Chandler describes the development of the mind as an increasing ability to "reason and discern truth consonant with the Word of God in order to nurture godly beliefs and a Christ-honoring worldview that reflects biblical knowledge, wisdom and understanding."[17]

Peter urges believers to "long for pure spiritual milk, that by it you may grow up into salvation—if indeed you have tasted that the Lord is good" (1 Pet. 2:2–3). God's Word is the "pure spiritual milk" Peter describes. God's Word, like spiritual milk, enables us to mature, or to "grow up into salvation." God's Word makes wise the simple (Ps. 19:7) and is the delight of maturing Christians (Ps. 1:2).

Our fundamental reason for existing is to worship God in Spirit and in truth. To worship God in truth means to worship him according to who he reveals himself to be in scripture. Biblical truth fuels worship, and worship enhances spiritual formation. Dallas Willard confirms, "To think of God rightly, as God is, one cannot help but lapse into worship; and worship is the single most powerful

---

[15] Hedges, 155.
[16] Piper, 41.
[17] Chandler, 21.

force in completing and sustaining the spiritual formation of the whole person."[18]

Truth is ultimately a Person

Jesus himself is the *Truth* that sets us free (Jn. 8:31–32). In Jesus's exchange with Pilate after his arrest, he says: "I have come into the world that I should bear witness to the truth. Everyone who is of the truth listens to my voice," to which Pilate dismissively responds, "What is truth?" (Jn. 18:37–38). Truth, for Christians, isn't simply principles or facts; truth is ultimately the person of Jesus Christ. Jesus, as the fullest revelation of God (Jn. 14:9), is the embodiment of truth. In nature, God's revelation is visualized, in scripture it is verbalized, and in Christ it is both.[19] The written Word of God is centered on the incarnate Word, Jesus. Pilate stares Truth in the face and walks away. As followers of Jesus, we cannot, like Pilate, walk away from the truth.

The apostle Peter reminds us that God has provided us with everything that pertains to life and godliness through the knowledge of Jesus Christ (2 Pet. 1:2–5). Therefore, we should "grow in the grace and knowledge of our Lord and Savior Jesus Christ" (2 Pet. 3:18), so that we can embody the truth to others. The light of God's grace "has shown in our hearts to give the light of the knowledge of the glory of God in the face of Jesus Christ" (2 Cor. 4:6). To drift away from truth is to drift away from Jesus. To drift away from Jesus is to drift away from the truth.

---

[18] Willard, 10.
[19] Stott, 29.

Pursuing Reason

In addition to truth, Christians must also pursue reason. Contrary to popular opinion, the Christian faith and reason are not in opposition to one another. Rather, they are intrinsically connected. God is a God of reason who calls us to rational faith (Is. 1:18). Faith and sight are contrasted in scripture (2 Cor. 5:7), but not faith and reason. John Stott says, "True faith is essentially reasonable because it trusts in the character and promises of God…faith and thought belong together, and believing is impossible without thinking."[20] While most other major religions are founded upon a person's unverifiable, or unreasonable, dream or vision, Christianity is inherently reasonable because it's founded upon truth.

The New Testament is full of good reasons for believing in Christ. Austin Farrar, Oxford theologian and New Testament scholar, believes C.S. Lewis's great success as a defender of Christianity was precisely because he demonstrated the reasonableness of the faith.[21] Not only did C.S. Lewis present the rationality of Christianity, so did Jesus himself.

Let's consider John 5 as a case study of how Jesus uses reasoning. In John 5, Jesus heals a man at the Pool of Bethesda on the Jewish Sabbath. The religious leaders aren't happy about this incident because it is against their laws to heal on the Sabbath. Not only does he heal on the Sabbath, but in the Pharisees' eyes, Jesus makes himself equal with God (Jn. 5:18). Rather than denying the Pharisees' conclusion, Jesus offers eleven reasons to confirm that he is indeed, equal with God. As noted by James Sire, Jesus explains the following in John 5:18–40:

1. I do what my Father does—give life to the dead (5:18–25)
2. I judge as a representative of the Father (5:22)

---

[20] Stott, 49–53.
[21] McGrath, 6.

3. If I am not honored, God is not honored (5:23)
4. The one who believes in me believes in God (5:24–27)
5. Like God, I have life in myself (5:26)
6. In God's power I always do what he wants (5:30)
7. John the Baptist testifies to who I am (5:31)
8. The "works" that I do testify to who I am (5:36)
9. The Father testifies to who I am (5:37)
10. The Scriptures testify to who I am (5:38)
11. Moses testifies to who I am (5:40)[22]

Jesus reasons with the Pharisees to verify he is equal with God. Jesus isn't our only biblical example of using reason. Paul "reasoned... from the Scriptures, explaining and proving that the Christ had to suffer and rise from the dead" (Acts. 17:2–3). In fact, Paul sums up his gospel ministry as "persuading others" of the truth (2 Cor. 5:11). Luke reports that Apollos "powerfully refuted the Jews in public, showing by the Scriptures that the Christ was Jesus" (Acts 18:28).

Like Jesus, Paul, and Apollos, all Christians are charged to use logic and reason to spread and defend the faith. Christians are commanded to be prepared to "make a defense to anyone who asks you for a reason for the hope that is in you..." (1 Pet. 3:15). If we neglect to use sound thought and reason to spread and defend the Christian faith, the faith will become weakened. James Orr expresses, "A religion divorced from earnest and lofty thought has always, down the whole history of the Church, tended to become weak...and unwholesome."[23] God's people must utilize sound reasoning to perpetuate the faith.

Although the Christian faith is reasonable, we must also accommodate paradox (or seeming contradiction) and mystery in our thinking. If we refuse to embrace paradox and mystery, we will

---

[22] James Sire, *Habits of the Mind: Intellectual Life as a Christian Calling* (Downers Grove, IL: InterVarsity Press, 2000), 191–192.

[23] James Orr, *The Christian View of God and the World* (Grand Rapids, MI: Eerdmans, 1954), 20–21.

miss some critical realities of Christianity. It may seem unreasonable that we experience abundant life by denying ourselves; it may seem irrational that we save our lives by losing them (Mt. 16:24–26; Jn. 10:10); it may seem illogical that we are fully responsible for our Christian growth and at the same time fully dependent upon God to give us the desire and ability to grow; but, these are all paradoxical realities according to scripture.

Thinking in *both/ands* instead of *either/ors* will help us accommodate mystery and avoid common errors in our thinking. For example, God is not *either* three *or* one, but *both* three *and* one; Jesus is not *either* fully God *or* fully man, but *both* fully God *and* fully man; God is not *either* sovereign *or* we are responsible, but God is *both* sovereign *and* we are responsible. You get the idea. Faithfulness to God requires us to use sound reasoning while humbly embracing the paradoxical realities and mysteries of scripture.

The Battle for the Mind

While pursuing the mind of Christ, we will face strong opposition. As referenced in Chapter Two, we are involved in a spiritual battle against the world, the flesh, and the devil. Because the mind is where transformation typically begins, it's also the battleground of spiritual warfare. When Satan decided to draw Eve away from God, he did not hit her with a stick, but with an idea.[24] If the enemy can penetrate one's mind, he can corrupt one's entire being.

Diane Chandler explains, "By gaining a stronghold in the mind, the enemy deposits doubt, confusion, fear and temptation in order to shift focus away from God and to foster disobedience…These destructive patterns of thinking become strongholds that need to be torn down…"[25] Since the fall of humanity, people have struggled

---

[24] Alan Andrews, ed., *The Kingdom Life: A Practical Theology of Discipleship and Spiritual Formation* (Colorado Springs, CO: NavPress, 2010), 49.
[25] Chandler, 145.

against sinful thought (Rom. 8:5–8), which expresses itself through a troubled mind (2 Kgs. 6:11), a depraved mind (1 Tim. 6:5), a dull mind (2 Cor. 3:14), a blinded mind (2 Cor. 4:4), a futile mind, a darkened mind, a foolish mind (Rom. 1:21), and a corrupted mind (2 Tim. 3:8). Sinful thinking is often the result of suppressing the truth of God (Rom. 1:18).

Christians are not immune to the effects of sin on the mind. For example, Jesus says to his disciples, "O foolish ones, and slow of heart to believe all that the prophets have spoken!" (Lk. 24:25). Paul says to the Galatians, "O foolish Galatians! Who has bewitched you?" (Gal. 3:1). Christians are susceptible to foolish and dangerous thinking. Therefore, in the battle for the mind, we must "test everything" (1 Thess. 5:21), make "spiritual" judgements about all things (1 Cor. 2:15), and "take every thought captive to obey Christ" (2 Cor. 3:5). In the context of 2 Corinthians 3:5, "every thought" doesn't merely refer to one's inward thoughts but to every external thought as well. External thoughts include all human wisdom, worldviews, and philosophies. Our digital and increasingly secular age has greatly expanded the horizon of thoughts that shape Christians.

God's Truth vs. Satan's Lies

God desires for his children to have a biblical worldview, or idea system, that reflects his truth and perspective. On the other hand, Satan wants to obscure the biblical worldview and lead people to ungodly idea systems. Since the fall, Satan and his demons have worked together to corrupt humanity through false philosophies (Col. 2:8), false religions (1 Cor. 10:20), false teachers (2 Cor. 11:14–15), false doctrine (1 Jn. 2:18), and false morals (2 Thess. 2:7–12).[26] The battle for the mind requires us to choose God's revealed truth over Satan's lies. Paul warns the Colossians, "See to it that no one takes you captive by philosophy and empty deceit, according to

---

[26] Gallaty, 85.

human tradition, according to the elemental spirits of the world, and not according to Christ" (Col. 2:8). The battle for a Christian mind requires us to recognize the empty deceit and evil idea systems that Satan uses to undermine God's truth. These corrupt idea systems include, but are not limited to:

- *Agnosticism*: The belief that it is impossible to know whether or not there is a God.
- *Anti-intellectualism*: A system of belief opposed to or hostile toward intellectuals and the modern academic, artistic, social, religious, and other theories associated with them.[27]
- *Atheism*: The belief that there is no God.
- *Consumerism*: The attachment to material values and things as a pathway to personal fulfillment.[28]
- *Deism*: This idea system promotes that God is revealed in nature, reflecting rationality and order, but he is neither personal nor sovereign over human affairs. Deism refutes that God has made himself known through creation, the Bible, and Jesus.[29]
- *Eastern philosophies*: In these pantheistic views, "God permeates the cosmos and exists in everything. Thus, the human soul is God."[30]
- *Humanism*: This worldview is divorced from faith in God. Rather, the human person becomes a god unto himself in exercising complete freedom of choice.[31]
- *Naturalism*: This approach to life exalts the mind and views matter, not God, as eternally existent in a cause-effect

[27] Dictionary.com, "Anti-intellectualism," accessed July 6, 2020, http://www.dictionary.com/browse/anti-intellectualism.
[28] Chandler, 143.
[29] Ibid., 141.
[30] Ibid., 142.
[31] Ibid., 142

relationship. Naturalism purports, "no god, no spirit, no life beyond the grave."[32]

- *New Age philosophy*: Eastern philosophies have birthed *New Age philosophy*, which involves various spiritualities that help one attain a higher consciousness through mystical experience.[33]

- *Nihilism*: Based on naturalism and humanism, nihilism presents a worldview that considers life as having no value or purpose. Believing there is no God, absolute truth, or moral standard, proponents of nihilism become a power unto themselves.[34]

- *Relativism*: This philosophy asserts that there is no absolute truth. Therefore, personal truth is the highest form of "truth" one can possess. The relativist says, "what's true for you is true for you; what's true for me is true for me."

- *Secularism:* The resistance of any kind of religious influence or expression in public life, especially relative to ethics.[35]

Unlike these deceitful, depressing, and false idea systems, the biblical worldview is rational, good, and true because it flows from the God of reason, goodness, and truth.

Alister McGrath notes, "Christianity offers an intellectual framework, a way of understanding and seeing our world, that makes sense of what is otherwise little more than a happy coincidence or an inexplicable (though fortunate) cosmic event."[36] Christians have the distinct privilege and opportunity to see the world through the lens of God's truth. C.S. Lewis affirms, "I believe in Christianity as I believe that the Sun has risen, not only because I see it, but because

---

[32] Chandler, 141.

[33] Ibid., 142.

[34] Ibid., 142.

[35] Ibid., 143.

[36] McGrath, 14.

DANIEL SPURGEON TANKERSLEY

by it, I see everything else."[37] In pursuing the mind of Christ, we must battle to maintain a biblical worldview.

A Battle Worth Fighting

In summary, to love God with our minds is to pursue the mind of Christ. To pursue the mind of Christ is to pursue his thought life, which includes truth and reason. Pursuing the mind of Christ requires Christians to battle the kingdom of darkness, but it's a battle worth fighting! Christlike thought is essential to holiness. However, we must realize that pursuing the mind of Christ is not an end in itself; God intends for the transformation of our minds to impact our hearts and hands, enhancing our overall spiritual formation. As we pursue the mind of Christ, let's pray like David: "Search me, O God, and know my heart! Try me and know my thoughts! And see if there be any grievous way in me, and lead me in the way everlasting!" (Ps. 139:23–24). And, let's remember this promise: "You keep him in perfect peace whose mind is stayed on you, because he trusts in you" (Is. 26:3).

---

[37] McGrath, 133.

DISCUSSION QUESTIONS:

Do you agree with Mark Noll's assessment that Christian Evangelicals are neglecting their minds? Why, or why not?

Why is the mind so important in spiritual formation?

How can a person pursue the mind of Christ?

What are some biblical commands regarding thought? Do you find some of these commands easier to obey than others? Explain.

Can you identify areas in your thought life where you have matured? What areas need improvement?

What does God's Word say about truth?

Is the Christian faith opposed to reason? Explain.

How would you rate yourself as a reasoner?

How is spiritual warfare related to pursuing the mind of Christ?

What are some dangerous worldviews and philosophies Christians should beware of?

5
CHAPTER

Heart: Pursuing the Inner Life of Christ

Keep your heart with all vigilance, for
from it flow the springs of life.
– Proverbs 4:23

Change that ignores the heart will seldom transform
the life. For a while, it may seem like the real thing,
but it will prove temporary and cosmetic.
– Paul David Tripp[1]

Spiritual formation occurs, in part, through the transformation of the heart. If a person's physical heart is unhealthy, his entire physical well-being is negatively affected. In the same way, if a person's spiritual heart is unhealthy, his overall spiritual formation is stifled. If a Christian neglects the heart, he or she distorts the faith God intends and hinders transformation into the image of Christ. Unless the heart changes, a person will not change. We cannot adequately reflect the mind of Christ or the hands of Christ if we

---

[1] Paul David Tripp, *Instruments in the Redeemer's Hands: People in Need of Change, Helping People in Need of Change* (Phillipsburg, NJ: P&R Publishing, 2002), 63.

neglect the heart of Christ. To love God with all your heart is to pursue the heart of Christ.

Scripture repeatedly bears witness to the natural depravity of the human heart (Jer. 17:9). The apostle Paul says that humanity's flawed thinking is "due to their hardness of heart" (Eph. 4:17–18). During his earthly ministry, Jesus frequently looked beyond human knowledge and outward appearance and got to the *heart* of matters. For example, he says about the Pharisees, "These people honor me with their lips, but their *hearts* are far from me" (Mt. 15:8, emphasis mine). In the Sermon on the Mount, Jesus says it's not just the murderer who is liable to judgment but anyone who is "angry with his brother" (Mt. 5:21–22). He says it's not just the person who commits adultery that sins but "everyone who looks...with lustful intent has already committed adultery...in his *heart*" (Mt. 5:27–28, emphasis mine). In this same sermon, Jesus calls his disciples to guard their hearts against hypocrisy, greed, worldliness, anxiety, self-righteousness, and judgment of others (Mt. 6:1–33; 7:1–5). Further still, he commands his followers to forgive from the heart (Mt. 18:35) and set their hearts on heaven (Mt. 6:19–21).

Thankfully, when a person is born again, he or she receives the decisive heart transplant needed for change to occur (Ezek. 36:26) — the dead, defective, loveless heart is exchanged with a new living heart. After receiving a new heart, Christians are able and required to seek, love, serve, obey, and turn to God with all their hearts (Deut. 4:29; 6:5; 10:12; 11:13; 13:3; 26:16; 30:2; 10). Given that Christians have new hearts, one may wonder if it's okay to "follow your heart." A Christian should follow the heart only so far as it's aligned with Christ's heart. Rather than giving us the wicked desires of our tainted hearts, God is concerned about aligning our hearts with his heart. As we delight in the Lord, his heart becomes our heart. Thus, David says, "Delight yourself in the Lord, and *he will give you the desires of your heart*" (Ps. 37:4, emphasis mine).

In Chapter Three, we defined the *heart* to represent one's inner self, or core. The inner self consists of one's affections, will, character, and emotions. Consequently, to pursue the heart of Christ is to seek his affections, will, character, and emotional health. Though we will examine the heart in four dimensions, keep in mind that these dimensions are interconnected and often overlap. Moreover, don't forget that the heart works in concert with the head and hands. Once again, Jesus, as the perfect human, is our standard because he alone fulfilled the Great Commandment by loving the Father with all of his heart.

In this chapter, we will discover the heart God wants us to develop by assessing the heart of Christ. We will expose Christ's heart by examining his affections, will, character, and emotional life. We will then discover how to pursue the heart of Christ. Even after a person is "in Christ," there is a constant need to align one's heart with the heart of Christ.

The Affections of Christ

When the Bible speaks of the heart, the focus is sometimes on the affections. For example, King David says, "Put no trust in extortion; set no vain hopes on robbery; if riches increase, set not your *heart* on them" (Ps. 62:10, emphasis mine). Jesus says, "For where your treasure is, there your *heart* will be also" (Mt. 6:21, emphasis mine). In response to Jesus interpreting the scriptures concerning himself, two of his disciples say to each other, "Did not our *hearts* burn within us while he talked to us on the road, while he opened to us the Scriptures?" (Lk. 24:32, emphasis mine). Paul says of the Philippians, "It is right for me to feel this way about you all, because I hold you in my *heart*, for you are all partakers with me of grace, both in my imprisonment and in the defense and confirmation of the gospel" (Phil. 1:7, emphasis mine).

In each of these verses, the word *heart* refers to the affections. In our culture, we often use the word *heart* to signify affections. For example, if you "put your heart" into something, you are affectionate about it. *Affections* are deep-seated inclinations that reflect one's love, passion, and devotion to objects, persons, or ideas.[2] Some affections are good, honorable, beneficial, and mature, while others are evil, destructive, selfish, and childish. Our goal as Christians is to develop the affections of Jesus.

Jesus is most affectionate about God the Father, God's people, and God's will. The Great Commandment and the Great Commission define the life and ministry of Jesus. As Christians, our primary affections should be the same. Like the psalmist, we should be able to say of God, "As a deer pants for flowing streams, so pants my soul for you, O God. My soul thirsts for God, for the living God" (Ps. 42:1–2). Like Paul, we should be able to say of God's people, "For God is my witness, how I yearn for you all with the affection of Christ Jesus" (Phil. 1:8). Like Jesus, we should be able to say of God's will, "My food is to do the will of him who sent me and to accomplish his work" (Jn. 4:34).

The affections of Christ can be called "holy affections." Jonathan Edwards famously stated, "Without holy affection there is no true religion."[3] Though our sinful affections often restrict us, they do not have to; God's grace enables us to overcome sinful affections and take on the affections of Christ.

The Will of Christ

When the Bible speaks of the heart, it's often emphasizing the will. For example, David prays, "Delight yourself in the Lord, and he will give you the desires of your *heart*" (Ps. 37:4, emphasis mine). The author of Hebrews says, "For the word of God is living and active,

---

[2] Dennis P. Hollinger, *Head, Heart & Hands: Bringing Together Christian Thought, Passion, and Action* (Downers Grove, IL: InterVarsity Press, 2005), 77.
[3] Jonathan Edwards as cited in Craig Troxel, *With All Your Heart: Orienting Your Mind, Desires, and Will Toward Christ* (Wheaton, IL: Crossway, 2020), 72.

sharper than any two-edged sword, piercing to the division of soul and of spirit, of joints and of marrow, and discerning the thoughts and intentions of the *heart*" (Heb. 4:12, emphasis mine). Regarding giving, Paul instructs the Corinthians, "Each one must give as he has decided in his *heart*..." (2 Cor. 9:7, emphasis mine).

In each of these examples, the word *heart* signifies the will. In conversation today, we often use the word *heart* to refer to the will. For example, if you have "a change of heart," you choose, or will, differently now. The *will* represents one's inner resolve and determination to act in certain ways. It's through the will that one consciously chooses to act or not to act toward certain ends.[4] The only person with a perfect will is Jesus.

The will of Jesus, reflected in his affections, is to please the Father by doing the Father's will. Jesus states, "I have come down from heaven, not to do my own will but the will of him who sent me...I always do what pleases him" (Jn. 6:38; 8:29). Even before going to the cross, Jesus prays to the Father, "Not my will, but yours be done" (Lk. 22:42). Jesus set the standard for us to follow by perfectly fulfilling the Father's will. Like Jesus, the Christian's will should be to carry out the will of the Father. Sanctification involves increasing and joyous devotion to God's will.

All Christians should pray, "Your kingdom come, your will be done, on earth as it is in heaven," and act accordingly (Mt. 6:10). Remember, Jesus says, "Not everyone who says to me, 'Lord, Lord,' will enter the kingdom of heaven, but the one who *does the will of my Father* who is in heaven" (Mt. 7:21, emphasis mine). He says, "whoever *does the will of my Father* in heaven is my brother and sister and mother" (Mt. 12:50, emphasis mine).

---

[4] Hollinger, 75.

General Will vs. Specific Will

When speaking of "God's will," it's helpful to distinguish his *general will* from his *particular will*. God's general will includes all people at all times while his particular will is for particular people at particular times. God's general will is revealed in scripture. His particular will is not explicitly revealed in scripture and includes things such as who you will marry, where you will work, how you will spend your money, and what you will eat for the next meal. Granted, God's Word provides the wisdom that guides us in these decisions, but it doesn't spell out the answers for us. Instead of beginning with the question, "What is God's will *for me?*," we should begin with the question, "What is God's will?" We are best able to discern God's particular will in the midst of obeying his general will. As we walk in God's general will day-by-day, the Holy Spirit will guide our decisions regarding his particular will.

God's general will for his people is that we seek first his kingdom and righteousness by loving him, loving people, and making disciples of Jesus. God wills for his people to be sanctified (1 Thess. 4:3), and led by the Spirit (Eph. 5:18). He desires for his people to serve him, obey him, and trust him. There isn't room in this short section to exhaust God's entire general will. However, if we spend time in his Word, our minds will be renewed, and we will be able to test and "discern what is the will of God, what is good and acceptable and perfect" (Rom. 12:2).

The night before Jesus dies, he prays to the Father, "I glorified you on earth, having accomplished the work that you gave me to do" (Jn. 17:4). There is no greater dying testament than that! May our daily confession and prayer be, "I delight to do your will, O my God; your law is within my heart… Turn my eyes from looking at worthless things; and give me life in your ways" (Ps. 40:8; 119:37).

The Character of Christ

When the Bible speaks of the heart, it's often referring to character. For example, the psalmist says, "Light is sown for the righteous, and joy for the upright in *heart*" (Ps. 97:11, emphasis mine). Jesus tells his followers, "Take my yoke upon you, and learn from me, for I am gentle and lowly in *heart*, and you will find rest for your souls" (Mt. 11:29, emphasis mine). He teaches his disciples, "The good person out of the good treasure of his *heart* produces good, and the evil person out of his evil treasure produces evil, for out of the abundance of the *heart* his mouth speaks" (Lk. 6:45, emphasis mine).

The word *heart* indicates character in these verses. In our language today, we often use the word *heart* to refer to character. For example, if someone says you "have a good heart," they are likely referring to your good character. *Character* reveals the virtues and morality of the heart; it is who we are when nobody's looking.[5] Robert Murray M'Cheyne highlighted the importance of character when he said, "What a man is alone on his knees before God, that he is, and no more."[6]

Jesus exhibits *and* describes the ideal character traits of a Christian. In the Sermon on the Mount, for example, Jesus says his followers will be marked by dependence on God, repentance, humility, righteousness, integrity, forgiveness, and faithfulness (Mt. 5:3–11). God's Word consistently dissuades bad character while exhorting Christlike character. For example, Paul tells the Christians of Galatia *not* to display sexual immorality, impurity, sensuality, idolatry, sorcery, enmity, strife, jealousy, fits of anger, rivalries, dissensions, division, envy, drunkenness, orgies, and "things like these" (Gal. 5:18–21). Contrasted with the list of things Christians *should not be*, is a list of things Christians *should be*. Paul says

---

[5] Hollinger, 86–88.

[6] Robert Murray M'Cheyne as cited in Nathan Busenitz, ed., *Right Thinking in a Church Gone Astray: Finding Our Way Back to Biblical Truth* (Eugene, OR: Harvest House Publishers, 2017), 167.

Christians *should be* loving, joyful, peaceful, patient, kind, good, faithful, gentle, and self-controlled. Those who belong to Christ should live by the Spirit and walk as Jesus walked (Gal.5:22–25).

Paul offers a list of representative Christlike character traits to Timothy. He tells Timothy a Christian should be above reproach, a one-woman man (or one-man woman), sober-minded, self-controlled, respectable, hospitable, gentle, temperate (not quarrelsome), generous (not a lover of money), a family leader, mature, humble, and respected by outsiders (1 Tim. 3:2–7). These character traits are required of elders, but they are not exclusive to elders because these traits are repeated elsewhere in scripture as qualities that should characterize all disciples of Christ.[7] Paul exhorts the Colossians to Christlike character as follows:

> Put on then, as God's chosen ones, holy and beloved, compassionate hearts, kindness, humility, meekness, and patience, bearing with one another and, if one has a complaint against another, forgiving each other; as the Lord has forgiven you, so you also must forgive. And above all these put on love, which binds everything together in perfect harmony. And let the peace of Christ rule in your hearts, to which indeed you were called in one body. And be thankful. (Col. 3:12–15)

God redeems his people so that they might reflect Jesus's character to the world. All Christians should bear the fruit of Christlike character (Jn. 15:8). Character matters because God doesn't simply want us to *desire* to be holy; he wants us to *be* holy (1 Pet. 1:15–16). We must reflect the character of Christ for our faith to be credible.

---

[7] Tim Challies, *The Character of the Christian* (Minneapolis, MN: Cruciform Press, 2017), 5.

The Emotional Life of Christ

When the Bible speaks of the heart, it's sometimes referring to a pattern of feeling or emotion. For example, scripture often uses the phrase *lose heart* to refer to discouragement (Lk. 18:1; 2 Cor. 4:1; 4:16; Eph. 3:13) and *take heart* to prompt courage (Mt. 9:2; 9:22; 14:27; Jn. 16:33; Acts 27:22; 25). When Aaron greets Moses, he is "glad in his heart" (Ex. 4:14). Peter commands Christians to have "a tender heart" (1 Pet. 3:8). Paul writes to the Corinthians out of much "anguish of the heart" (2 Cor. 2:4).

In our culture, we often use the word *heart* in reference to emotions as well. For example, if a person is emotionally cold and insensitive, they may be called "heartless." If you "wear your heart on your sleeve," your emotional state is apparent. *Emotions* (or feelings) can be defined as overarching patterns of "pleasurable or painful sensations we experience in response to particular events, objects, people or ideas."[8] Emotions express the things we love and value, whether we understand them or not.[9] Peter Scazzero observes, "Emotional health and spiritual maturity are inseparable. It is not possible to be spiritually mature while remaining emotionally immature."[10]

God describes himself in scripture as a God of emotion, and he intends for humanity, created in his image, to reflect his emotions. Our emotions allow us to share God's heart, purpose, and perspective.[11] Due to sin, our emotions do not always reflect reality. For example, we may not always *feel* God's presence with us, but that does not change the reality that he is with us always. As part of our transformation into the image of Christ, our emotions need

---

[8] Hollinger, 78.

[9] Alasdair J. Groves and Winston T. Smith, *Untangling Emotions: God's Gift of Emotions* (Wheaton, IL: Crossway, 2019), 35.

[10] Peter Scazzero, *The Emotionally Healthy Church: A Strategy for Discipleship that Actually Changes Lives* (Grand Rapids, MI: Zondervan, 2010), 10.

[11] Groves and Smith, 27.

renovation. Restoration of the emotional life happens as we pursue the emotional life of Jesus.

Jesus boldly and freely expressed his emotions while on Earth. Jesus shed tears (Lk. 19:41), was filled with joy (Lk. 10:21), grieved (Mk. 14:34), got angry (Mk. 3:5), experienced sadness (Mt. 26:37), felt compassion (Lk. 7:13), experienced sorrow (Jn. 11:35), showed astonishment and wonder (Mk. 6:6; Lk. 7:9), felt distressed (Mk. 3:5; Lk. 12:50), and longed to be with his disciples (Lk. 22:15). Jesus did not ignore or suppress his emotions, indicating that emotional engagement is a sign of spiritual maturity. Jesus perfectly expressed both positive emotions such as happiness, joy, and peace, and negative emotions such as anger, disgust, and sadness.

To be clear, Jesus never exhibited sinful emotions, only the necessary negative emotions. Negative emotions are required in a world full of sin and evil. We *should* be angry at sin and sad about death. To suppress or ignore sadness and grief is unwise and unhealthy. Thankfully, a day is coming when negative emotions will not be necessary. But, as long as we live in a broken world, negative emotions are required and must be embraced.

Emotions cannot be turned on and off at will. Rather, they must be dealt with at the source. As Christians, we must engage our own emotions *and* the emotions of others in the body of Christ. Paul says, "If one member suffers, all suffer together; if one member is honored, all rejoice together" (1 Cor. 12:26). To the Romans, he writes, "rejoice with those who rejoice, weep with those who weep" (Rom. 12:15). Loving others requires us to engage in their experiences and emotions with them.

Jesus, though he had perfect emotional health, consistently took his emotions to God through prayer, and we must do the same. We need God's help and guidance as we identify, examine, evaluate, and act on our emotions. We need God's help to look beneath the surface of our lives, break the power of how our past influences our present, live in brokenness and vulnerability, know our limits, embrace loss and grief, make Jesus our model for living well, and slow down in order to live lives of integrity.[12] We need God to give us the ability to express the appropriate emotion at the appropriate time. We need God to help us develop the emotional health of Jesus.

Nurturing the Heart Through Spiritual Disciplines

Now that we have examined the heart God wants us to have, let's consider *how* we can pursue the heart of Christ. We cannot, in the moment and by direct effort, change our hearts. We cannot simply adjust a dial and control our affections, will, character, or mood. To try to change the heart in the moment by direct willpower is to misunderstand how the heart works. Dallas Willard points out that we cannot behave "on the spot" as Jesus did unless we live the way Jesus did before the "spot" got there; we cannot genuinely reflect Jesus's heart in the difficult moments of life unless we adopt his overall lifestyle.[13] Adopting Jesus's lifestyle requires us to live a life of spiritual discipline.

Spiritual disciplines are activities within our power that enable us, by God's grace, to do what we cannot do by direct effort.[14] Though we cannot, in the moment and by direct effort, love our enemies or bless those who curse us, Willard notes, "by a wise practice of disciplines in the presence of Christ, we can become people who will routinely and easily do so."[15] Tim Keller confirms, "When New Testament writers say, 'Love your neighbor as yourself,' they're saying, 'nurture that new nature inside you so you can love your neighbor as yourself.'"[16] Through spiritual disciplines, we

---

[12] Scazzero, 18.

[13] Dallas Willard, *The Spirit of the Disciplines: Understanding How God Changes Lives* (San Francisco, CA: Harper and Row, 1988), 7.

[14] Dallas Willard, *Renewing the Christian Mind: Essays, Interviews, and Talks* (New York, NY: HarperCollins Publishers, 2016), 283.

[15] Ibid., 283

[16] Tim Keller, *On Birth* (New York, NY: Penguin Books, 2020), 91.

can nurture our new nature so that we naturally reflect the heart of Christ. In the same way a well-nurtured apple tree will easily and naturally produce apples, a well-nurtured heart will easily and naturally produce the fruit of Christlikeness.

Robert Mulholland Jr. notes in his classic book *Invitation to a Journey*, "Just as a journey from one place to another requires varied sets of disciplines for successful completion (walking, driving, flying, navigation skills and the like), so the Christian journey has its own sets of disciplines which enable the pilgrim to progress... toward wholeness in Christ."[17] Like a marriage or excelling in a particular career path or sport, being a Christian involves hard work, faithfulness, and perseverance. It's no wonder the apostle Paul compares a Christian to an athlete in training. Paul tells Timothy, "train yourself for godliness; for while bodily training is of some value, godliness is of value in every way, as it holds promise for the present life and also for the life to come" (1 Tim. 4:7–8). As physical discipline promotes physical health, spiritual discipline promotes godliness. The path to sanctification includes discipline; there is no shortcut.

There is no precise number of spiritual disciplines. Some people limit the disciplines to a select few, while others consider anything God commands to be a spiritual discipline. The spiritual disciplines include, but are not limited to: Bible intake, prayer, corporate worship, evangelism, discipleship, service, proper stewardship, fasting, solitude, and fellowship. While the spiritual disciplines can be approached in various ways, Richard Averbeck notes that a helpful approach is to divide the disciplines into two categories, corresponding to human breathing:

> Like human breathing for physical life, doing spiritual life with God and one another requires

---

[17] Robert Mulholland, *Invitation to a Journey: A Road Map for Spiritual Formation* (Downers Grove, IL: InterVarsity Press, 2016), 89.

an ongoing pattern of breathing in and breathing out. There is a life-giving dynamic relationship between them: (1) *inhaling*: breathing in from God by reading, studying, memorizing, and meditating on Scripture; solitude and silence; fasting; and (2) *exhaling*: breathing out toward God and others through prayer and worship; fellowship, service, and mission; living the fruit of the Spirit. Like physical breathing, doing one without the other is to lose life.[18]

Luke recorded in Acts 2:42–47 that the early church disciples modeled all types of disciplines. They were committed to scripture intake, fellowship, prayer, praise and worship, and outreach. Regardless of how we choose to approach the disciplines, we must agree that they are absolutely necessary for heart change.

The Primary Spiritual Disciplines

Eugene Peterson likens the spiritual disciplines to a set of garden tools because some disciplines require daily practice, while others may be used less frequently. Bill Hull notes that Peterson "saw the soil of a garden as the human soul, the rain and sunshine as the staple disciplines such as interaction with the Scriptures and prayer. The other tools are over in the shed, used when it's time to till, weed, plant, or do some other task."[19] The "other tools" used only at certain times include disciplines such as fasting or serving. In agreement with Peterson, I believe the two most important disciplines are Bible intake and prayer. Bible intake is the ultimate *inhaling* of God, while

---

[18] Alan Andrews, ed., *The Kingdom Life: A Practical Theology of Discipleship and Spiritual Formation* (Colorado Springs, CO: NavPress, 2010), 288.

[19] Bill Hull, *Choose the Life: Exploring a Faith that Embraces Discipleship* (Grand Rapids, MI: Baker Books, 2004), 67.

prayer is the ultimate *exhaling* to God. Charles Spurgeon said, "When asked, 'what is more important: Praying or reading the Bible?' I ask, 'What is more important, breathing in or breathing out?'"

Bible intake

According to the American Bible Society, the number one predictor of spiritual growth is "engaging scripture."[20] As we engage scripture, it sanctifies us by renewing our minds (Rom. 12:2), teaching, reproofing, correcting, and training us in righteousness (2 Tim. 3:16–18). Scripture reveals how to honor God in all areas of life, including singleness, marriage, parenting, vocation, and financial stewardship.

We can ask ourselves all day, "What would Jesus do?" But, if we don't know scripture, we will not have an answer. There are five primary ways to intake, or engage, the Bible. We can hear the Word (Lk. 11:28; Rom. 10:17), read the Word (e.g., Rev. 1:3), study the Word (e.g., Ezr. 7:10; Acts 17:11), memorize the Word (Ps. 119:11; Prov. 22:17–19), and meditate on the Word (Ps. 1:1–2; 19:14; 119:15). As we intake scripture, the Spirit helps us understand and apply it to our lives.

Unfortunately, God's Word is often misunderstood, taken out of context, and abused. It's possible to twist God's Word to make it say almost anything we want it to say. As an extreme example, consider this: the Bible says, "there is no God." That's a true statement. Psalm 14:1 begins, "*The fool says in his heart*, 'there is no God'" (emphasis mine). Can you see why context matters? It's no wonder Paul commands young Timothy to show himself approved by "rightly dividing the word of truth" (2 Tim. 2:15).

To properly intake the Word of God, we must adopt a sound method, such as the Inductive Bible Study Method popularized

---

[20] Jared Wilson, *The Gospel-Driven Church: Uniting Church Growth Dreams with the Metrics of Grace* (Grand Rapids, MI: Zondervan, 2019), 80.

by Kay Arthur.[21] The Inductive Method is a threefold process that includes observation (What does the text say?), explanation (What does the text mean?), and application (How does the text apply to me?). The Inductive Method, or other appropriate methods, will help us arrive at God's intended meaning and purpose of any given scripture.

Prayer

Prayer is *personal communication with God.*[22] Only through Jesus, our perfect mediator, do we have access to God in prayer (1 Tim. 4:5). Prayer is critical to the Christian life for at least four major reasons. First of all, prayer matters because God commanded us to pray (Mt. 6:9; 1 Thess. 5:17; Phil. 4:6; Col. 4:2). Secondly, prayer matters because Jesus modeled a life of prayer (Lk. 5:16; Mk. 1:35; Mt. 14:23). Tim Keller explains:

> Jesus taught his disciples to pray, healed people with prayers, denounced the corruption of the temple worship (which, he said, should be a house of prayer), and insisted that some demons could be cast out only through prayer...The Holy Spirit came upon Him as he was praying, and he was transfigured with the divine glory as he prayed. When he faced His greatest crisis, he did so with prayer. We hear him praying for his disciples and the church on the night before he died and then petitioning God in

---

[21] Kay Arthur, *How to Study Your Bible* (Eugene, OR: Harvest House Publishers 1992).

[22] Wayne Grudem, *Systematic Theology: An Introduction to Biblical Doctrine* (Grand Rapids, MI: Zondervan, 1994), 376.

agony in the Garden of Gethsemane. Finally, he
died praying.[23]

Of all the things Jesus's disciples could have asked him to teach
them, they ask Jesus to teach them to pray (Lk. 11:1). Thirdly, prayer
matters because God responds to prayer (Ps. 40:1; Jer. 33:3; 5:16;
Lk. 11:9–13). James bluntly states, "you do not have, because you do
not ask" (Js. 4:2). We should all consider what blessings God might
want to give us that we have not asked for. Finally, prayer matters
because God ordains prayer as a means to accomplish his purposes.
(Mt. 9:37–38; Jer. 29:11–14).

To pray effectively, we should pray according to God's will. The
goal of prayer is not to align God's will with our will, but to align our
will with God's perfect will. James addresses misguided prayer when
he says, "You ask and do not have because you ask wrongly" (Js. 4:3).
We ask rightly by praying according to God's Word. Effective prayer
also requires faith (Js. 1:5–8; Mk. 11:24; Mt. 21:22). Faith should
not be in the power of our prayers. Instead, faith should be in the
power of the One we pray to.

Finally, prayer is most effective in the context of obedience. John
says, "Beloved, if our heart does not condemn us, we have confidence
before God; and whatever we ask we receive from him, because we
keep his commandments and do what pleases him" (1 Jn. 3:21–22).
If we walk in obedience to God's commands, our hearts will not
condemn us, and we can be confident God will hear our prayers.
James confirms, "The prayer of a *righteous* person has great power as
it is working" (Js. 5:16, emphasis mine). On the contrary, if we walk
in deliberate disobedience and unrighteousness, God will not listen
to our prayers (Ps. 66:18).

Our prayer lives should include prayers of thanksgiving (1
Thess. 5:18), prayers of confession (1 Jn. 1:9), prayers of petition for

---

[23] Tim Keller, *Prayer: Experiencing Awe and Intimacy with God* (New York,
NY: Penguin Group, 2014), 27.

ourselves (1 Jn. 5:14–15), and prayers of intercession for the needs of others (Eph. 6:18–19). Prayer is a divine gift that changes things, changes us, and unites us with God himself.

The Spiritual Disciplines Must Be
Grounded in God's Grace

Human nature causes us to turn spiritual growth into a do-it-yourself operation. Unfortunately, a self-sufficient mindset misses the gospel of God's grace. *Grace* can be defined as "God acting in our lives to accomplish what we can't accomplish on our own."[24] Robert Mulholland Jr. highlights the tension between God's grace and human performance of the spiritual disciplines:

> Since the disciplines are activities we perform, from the very first performance there is the possibility that we will begin to think our performance will make the difference in our growth...there is a tremendous tension here. Without our performance of the disciplines, God is for all practical purposes, left without any means of grace through which to effect transformation in our lives. But without God's transforming grace, our disciplines are empty, hollow motions, the form of godliness without power.[25]

The solution to the grace/performance tension is to practice the spiritual disciplines while being grounded in the gospel of God's grace. Otherwise, the disciplines become legalistic and self-centered instead of God-centered. Author John Koessler explains, "Effort is incompatible with grace when that effort is seen as a means of

---

[24] Andrews, 51.
[25] Mulholland, 57.

earning God's acceptance. When my efforts become the basis for my confidence with God, rather than the work of Christ, I have crossed over into the realm of legalism."[26] A legalistic approach to spiritual discipline leads to either pride due to good performance, or despair due to bad performance.

The spiritual disciplines have no value in themselves. Their value is that they are means of God's grace as they put us in a position to know God, enjoy him, and be transformed by him. Greg Ogden clarifies, "The spiritual disciplines are like sails on a boat. Only God can provide the wind of His Spirit to ignite the impetus for movement, but we can hoist the sails to be ready when God decides to move in and through us."[27] We cannot provide the power to transform our hearts; only God can do that. Our responsibility is to put up the sails and expect God's blessing and transforming power.

The Most Disciplined Person Who Ever Lived

Jesus Christ, our example, is the most disciplined person ever to live. Yet, he is also the most joyful person ever to live. When we understand the spiritual disciplines as Jesus's invitation to a better way of living, as opposed to burdensome commands, we are able to find freedom and rest for our souls (Mt. 11:29–30). Elizabeth Elliot says, "Freedom and discipline have come to be regarded as mutually exclusive, when in fact, freedom is not at all the opposite, but the final reward of discipline."[28] With the proper perspective, the spiritual disciplines become a delight instead of drudgery. Without exception, godly people are spiritually disciplined people. By God's

---

[26] John Koessler, *True Discipleship: The Art of Following Jesus* (Chicago, IL: Moody Publishers, 2003), 114.

[27] Greg Ogden, *The Essential Commandment: A Disciple's Guide to Loving God and Others* (Downers Grove, IL: InterVarsity Press, 2011), 122.

[28] Donald Whitney, *Spiritual Disciplines for the Christian Life* (Colorado Springs, CO: NavPress, 1997), 21.

grace, through the practice of spiritual disciplines, a Christian can experience a change of heart. I pray, "the Lord [will] cause you to increase and abound in love, so that He may establish your hearts without blame in holiness before our God and Father" (1 Thess. 3:12–13).

DISCUSSION QUESTIONS:

Why is heart change necessary for genuine transformation to occur?

What is the *heart*?

How would you describe the affections of Christ?

How would you describe the will of Christ?

How would you describe the character of Christ?

How would you describe the emotional life of Christ?

In which of these areas do you most need to mature? Explain.

How can a person pursue the heart of Christ?

What spiritual disciplines do you need to implement in your life?

Why must the spiritual disciplines be grounded in God's grace?

Do you find the spiritual disciplines to be burdensome? If so, how can you change your perspective on them?

6

CHAPTER

Hands: Pursuing the Actions of Christ

By this we may know that we are in him: whoever says he abides
in him ought to walk in the same way in which he walked.
– 1 John 2:5–6

The shortest distance between us and the life
we long for is total obedience to Christ.
– Max Anders[1]

Active obedience is indispensable to Christianity. To love God with all our strength is to move into the physical realm and pursue the *hands*, or actions, of Christ. The *hands* represent one's active obedience to God and good works toward others. Throughout Christian history, much has been written about the merits of thought and faith versus the need for action. Ultimately, Christianity embraces thought *and* action; faith *and* works. A person may have great biblical knowledge and overflow with affection and emotion, but if faith is not expressed through action and obedience, it's not genuine faith. James says Christians should be "*doers* of the

---

[1] Max Anders, *Brave New Discipleship: Cultivating Scripture-Driven Christians in a Culture-Driven World* (Nashville, TN: Thomas Nelson, 2015), 16.

word, and not hearers only" because faith without works is dead (Js. 1:22; 2:17, emphasis mine). Paul says Christians should "*walk* in a manner worthy of the God who calls [us] into His own kingdom and glory" (1 Thess. 2:12, emphasis mine).

Furthermore, Jesus tells his followers, "If you love me you will *obey* my commandments" (Jn. 14:15, emphasis mine). He says, "Everyone then who hears these words of mine and *does them* will be like a wise man who built his house on the rock" (Mt. 7:24, emphasis mine). The essence of the Great Commission is to teach Christians to *do* all Jesus commands. To understand just how necessary active obedience is in the Christian life, we do not have to look any further than John 3:36: "Whoever believes in the Son has eternal life; whoever *does not obey* the Son shall not see life, but the wrath of God remains on him" (emphasis mine).

God does not save his people simply so they will think rightly and feel rightly, but so that they will *act* rightly. Salvation apart from obedience is foreign to God's design. Scripture goes so far as to say that Christians are no longer controlled by sin; rather, they are "slaves of righteousness" (Rom. 6:17–18). We should not expect to know God, experience him, or represent him properly apart from obedience to his commands.

Regarding the interrelation of the head, heart, and hands, we should obey God whether we feel like it or not. Obeying God when we do not feel like it can be an act of faith in and of itself.[2] Furthermore, our lack of understanding is not a valid excuse to disobey God's clear commands. Sometimes obedience actually precedes understanding in the walk of faith.

Significant damage is done to Christianity when professing Christians disobey Jesus. Pastor Dave Browning observes, "the gap holding back most believers is not the gap between what they know and what they don't know. It's the gap between what they know

---

[2] JD Greear, *Gospel: Recovering the Power that Made Christianity Revolutionary* (Nashville, TN: B&H Publishing, 2011), 98.

and what they're living. Many Christians are...educated beyond their obedience."[3] When professing Christians disobey Christ and conform to the sinful pattern of the world, the world is repulsed by our hypocrisy and alleges that Christianity has nothing to offer. Mahatma Gandhi, the most significant Hindu of the twentieth century, famously said, "I consider Western Christianity in its practical working a negation of Christ's Christianity."[4] Ouch! In order to reclaim and perpetuate "Christ's Christianity," we must *act* according to God's will. In this chapter, we will discover that active obedience involves imitating Christ, doing good works, and caring for our physical bodies. We will also see that God gracefully rewards obedience!

The Imitation of Christ

We express our genuine faith in Christ through our imitation of Christ. Throughout human existence, psychologists, sociologists, educators, and anthropologists have emphasized the vital role of imitation. To be human is to be an imitator.[5] To be a Christian is to imitate Christ. The call to imitate Christ runs throughout the New Testament. Christ himself commands his disciples, "follow me" (Mt. 4:19), and "learn from me" (Mt. 11:29). The most direct comment from Jesus regarding imitation of him is when he washes the disciples' feet. Jesus says, "I have given you an example, that you also should do just as I have done to you" (Jn. 13:15).

---

[3] Dave Browning, *Deliberate Simplicity: How the Church Does More by Doing Less* (Grand Rapids, MI: Zondervan, 2009, Kindle Electronic Edition), 515–518.

[4] Robert Ellsberg, ed., *Gandhi on Christianity* (Maryknoll, NY: Orbis, 1991), 32.

[5] Kenneth O. Gangel and James C. Wilhoit, eds., *The Christian Educator's Handbook on Spiritual Formation* (Wheaton, IL: Victor Books, 1994), 205–206.

Paul urges the Corinthians, "Be imitators of me, as I am of Christ" (1 Cor. 11:1). John says, "By this we may know that we are in him: whoever says he abides in him ought to walk in the same way in which he walked" (1 Jn. 2:5–6). The biblical evidence is clear that Jesus, particularly in his earthly life, is our example. Every Christian should be able to say to other Christians, "Imitate me as I imitate Christ" (1 Cor. 11:1). As we imitate Jesus, we become more like him.

I am not advocating that we should do everything Jesus did (do not attempt to walk on water or control the weather!). But, I am advocating that we should attempt to do everything we are called by God to do *in the manner* and *from the source* from which Jesus did all that he did.[6] Christians today should do what Jesus would do were he living his life through us.[7] Imitating Christ today includes three dimensions: (1) learning to do the things that Jesus explicitly said do; (2) learning to conduct the usual activities of life in the character and power of Jesus; (3) learning to exercise the power of the kingdom to minister good and defeat evil in all of the connections of earthly existence.[8]

Created for Good Works

The apostle Paul makes it clear that people are not justified by good works, but by Jesus Christ (Gal. 2:16; Eph. 2:8–9). However, that does not mean Christians should not do good works. Paul explicitly states that Christians are created "*for good works*, which God prepared beforehand, that we should *walk in them*" (Eph. 2:10, emphasis mine). Good works display God. Jesus, the one we imitate,

---

[6] Dallas Willard, *Renewing the Christian Mind: Essays, Interviews, and Talks* (New York, NY: Harper One, 2016), 23.

[7] Steven Porter, Gary Moon, and J.P. Moreland, *Until Christ is Formed in You: Dallas Willard and Spiritual Formation* (Abilene, TX: Abilene Christian University Press, 2018), 188.

[8] Willard, 281–283.

"went about doing good" (Acts 10:38), and we must do the same. Christ enables us to put sin to death and pour ourselves into good deeds of righteousness (1 Pet. 2:24).

James explains through the example of Abraham that faith is always accompanied by works (2:21), is active alongside works (2:22), and is completed by works (2:22). Interestingly, every record of faith from the Old Testament recorded in Hebrews 11 is accompanied by an action: Abel offered a sacrifice to God; Noah built an ark; Abraham went out in the face of uncertainty; Sarah bore a child in her old age; Moses's parents hid him for three months despite the king's edict; Rahab gave a friendly welcome to the spies.[9] Faith and works cannot be separated.

God desires for his children to stir one another up to good works (Heb. 10:24), not grow weary in doing good (Gal. 6:9), be ready for every good work (2 Tim. 2:21), be a model of good works (2 Tim. 2:7), be zealous for good works (Tit. 2:14), be devoted to good works (Tit. 3:8,14), bear fruit in every good work (Col. 1:10), use their spiritual gifts to do good to one another (1 Pet. 4:10), and entrust their souls to God while doing good (1 Pet. 4:19). Expressing what we call the "Golden Rule," Jesus says, "whatever you wish that others would do to you, do also to them, for this is the Law and the Prophets" (Mt. 7:12). Paul explains that good works should be aimed at both Christians and non-Christians. He says, "As we have opportunity, let us do good to *everyone*, and especially to those who are of the household of faith" (Gal. 6:10, emphasis mine).

Jesus exemplifies that doing good includes meeting both physical needs and spiritual needs. Matthew states, "Jesus went throughout all the cities and villages, *teaching* in their synagogues and proclaiming the gospel of the kingdom and *healing* every disease and every affliction" (Mt. 9:35, emphasis mine). Good works may include praying, giving, serving, orphan care, adoption, speaking

---

[9] Robby Gallaty, *Bearing Fruit: What Happens When God's People Grow* (Nashville, TN: B&H, 2017), 103.

truth, advocating for justice, engaging in social, political, and cultural issues, or countless other acts. Of all the good works one can do, there is no greater work than discipleship. Most good works actually fall under the umbrella of discipleship, which is the topic of the next chapter.

Good Works as Evidence of Salvation

Matthew 25 contains a sobering account of the importance of good works. In this passage, Jesus describes the Final Judgement in which he will separate believers from non-believers:

> When the Son of Man comes in his glory, and all the angels with him, then he will sit on his glorious throne. Before him will be gathered all the nations, and he will separate people one from another as a shepherd separates the sheep from the goats... the King will say to those on his right, "Come, you who are blessed by my Father, inherit the kingdom prepared for you from the foundation of the world. For I was hungry and you gave me food, I was thirsty and you gave me drink, I was a stranger and you welcomed me, I was naked and you clothed me, I was sick and you visited me, I was in prison and you came to me... Truly, I say to you, as you did it to one of the least of these my brothers, you did it to me." Then he will say to those on his left, "Depart from me, you cursed, into the eternal fire prepared for the devil and his angels. For I was hungry and you gave me no food, I was thirsty and you gave me no drink, I was a stranger and you did not welcome me, naked and you did not clothe me, sick and in prison and you did not visit me...Truly, I say to you,

as you did not do it to one of the least of these, you did not do it to me." And these will go away into eternal punishment, but the righteous into eternal life. (Mt. 25:31–46)

Jesus describes genuine believers as people who do good works for the needy, sick, and outcast. He describes non-believers as people who neglect to do so.

James echoes Jesus as he commands Christians to display their faith by caring for the widows, orphans, poor, disadvantaged, and oppressed (Js. 1:27). The apostle Paul confirms the importance of good works as evidence of salvation: "He will render to each one according to his *works*: to those who by patience in well-doing seek for glory and honor and immortality, he will give eternal life; but for those who are self-seeking and do not obey the truth, but obey unrighteousness, there will be wrath and fury" (Rom. 2:6–8, emphasis mine). In a world full of need, Christians have endless opportunities to do good to others. If we simply put into practice the good works God commands, most of the problems that trouble the world would be eliminated.[10]

Good Works are for God's Glory

Ultimately, we do good works not so people will be helped, but so the world will see our good works and give glory to God (Mt. 5:16). Paul affirms, "whatever you do, *do all to the glory of God*" (1 Cor. 10:31, emphasis mine). As we walk in the good works God prepared for us, we should realize they are an outflow of God's grace to us, as opposed to opportunities for us to earn God's favor. It is God who works in us both to will and to work for his good pleasure (Phil. 2:13). To God be the glory!

---

[10] Willard, 265.

Glorify God in Your Body

The Great Divide

Obedience to God includes not only good works but control over our physical bodies. Ancient Greek dualistic thinking incorrectly viewed the spiritual life as separate from and superior to the physical life. Dr. Gregg Allison claims that contemporary evangelicalism also suffers from a divide between the spiritual and the physical. Evangelical Christians are engaged in meeting the spiritual needs of others, but at the same time:

> medical and sociological statistics bear witness to the fact that of all the religious traditions, conservative Protestants are the most overweight... Contributors to this plight include poor nutrition, overconsumption of food, absent or irregular physical exercise, lack of rest and leisure, poor sleep patterns, and more.[11]

Author Ruth Haley Barton describes her struggle with the "great divide" as follows: "Intent on trying to be 'spiritual,' for years I thought my body warranted little attention. As long as warning lights weren't flashing, I could ignore it in favor of more spiritual endeavors."[12] She later discovered that the physical life and the spiritual life are "inescapably intertwined."[13] Ironically, every "spiritual" discipline requires bodily action.

---

[11] Christopher Morgan, ed., *Biblical Spirituality* (Wheaton, IL: Crossway, 2019), 241.

[12] Greg Ogden, *The Essential Commandment: A Disciple's Guide to Loving God and Others* (Downers Grove, IL: InterVarsity Press, 2011), 145.

[13] Ogden, 145.

The Christian Life Is an Embodied Life

Jesus modeled that the body matters because the spiritual life is an embodied life.[14] Whenever we act for good or for evil, we do so with our bodies because God created us as bodily creatures. The greatest evidence for the dignity and importance of the physical body is found in the Incarnation of Jesus Christ. Jesus, though he is God, took on a human body. He was born as a baby and matured physically (Lk. 2:52). He was subject to physical human weaknesses such as hunger and weariness (Mt. 4:2; Jn. 4:6). When Jesus prayed, "give us this day our daily bread," he was asking God for everything his body needed (Mt. 6:11). Jesus never devalued the human body. Instead, he controlled and cared for his body perfectly.

The apostle Paul regularly addresses the embodied life. He speaks of his body as an adversary that, if left unchecked, will war against his soul (1 Cor. 9:27). He appeals to Christians, "by the mercies of God out of the mercies of God, to *present your bodies as a living sacrifice,* holy and acceptable to God, which is your spiritual worship" (Rom. 12:1, emphasis mine). He says, "do you not know that your body is a temple of the Holy Spirit within you, whom you have from God? You are not your own, for you were bought with a price. So glorify God in your body" (1 Cor. 6:19–20). Our bodies are God's, purchased through the blood of Christ.

Greg Ogden states, "Like athletes training for competition, farmers preparing for a harvest or soldiers under orders (2 Timothy 2:3–6), lovers of God bring their spirit *and body* under self-mastery in order to align all of their efforts toward fulfilling God's purpose for their life."[15] Spiritual disciplines are most important to the Christian because they benefit us in this life *and* the life to come. However, the apostle Paul made it clear that physical disciplines, or

---

[14] John Koessler, *True Discipleship: The Art of Following Jesus* (Chicago, IL: Moody Publishers, 2003), 95.

[15] Ogden, 123.

embodied disciplines, are "of some value" in this life (1 Tim. 4:7–8). Embodied disciplines include regular exercise, a good diet, sexual purity, and proper rest, among other things.[16]

Discipline of the body enhances physical health, which enables one to carry out God's will more effectively. Diane Chandler notes, "As a conduit for God's glory, the body can be developed to maximize its purpose...Informed physical health stewardship, in contrast to idolatry of the body, optimizes Kingdom effectiveness."[17] Embracing the embodied disciplines causes one's health, relationships, work, ministry, and relationship with God to flourish.

Glorified Bodies

Sin thwarts God's original intent for our bodies. Though God created the first humans to live forever in bodily perfection, sin now causes our physical bodies to weaken, disfunction, decay, and eventually return to dust (Gen. 3:19). One day, God will reverse the effects of sin on our bodies permanently and provide us with glorified bodies (1 Cor. 15:42–44)! We, like Jesus, will live eternally in a perfected and glorified body. Given the importance of the body, any approach to Christian spiritual formation that ignores the body is simply unbiblical. Based on God's design and intent for the body, Christians should aim to be the purest and healthiest of all people.

God Rewards Good Works

James describes life on earth as "a mist that appears for a little time and then vanishes" (Js. 4:14). After our brief time on earth ends,

---

[16] Morgan, ed., 253.

[17] Diane Chandler, *Christian Spiritual Formation: An Integrated Approach for Personal and Relational Wholeness* (Downers Grove, IL: InterVarsity Press, 2014), 181–183.

"we must all appear before the judgment seat of Christ, so that each one may receive what is due for what he has done in the body, whether good or evil" (2 Cor. 5:10). The "judgment seat of Christ" does not reveal one's salvation, but one's heavenly reward. In other words, present-day actions have eternal consequences. G-ood works done with a right heart gain eternal rewards! Jesus motivates his followers to store up treasure in heaven by faithfully following him on earth (Mt. 6:19–21). As we imitate Jesus, do good works, and honor God with our bodies, we store up eternal rewards. Randy Alcorn notes that Jesus, of course, is our first treasure, heaven is our second treasure, and power (Lk.19:15–19), possessions (Mt. 19:21), and pleasures (Ps. 16:11) are our third treasure.[18] In an astonishing display of God's grace, though *he* is the one who works in and through us, he rewards *us* for the work! Paul reminds Christians, "Whatever you do, work heartily, as for the Lord and not for men, knowing that from the Lord *you will receive the inheritance as your reward*. You are serving the Lord Christ (Col. 3:22–24, emphasis mine).

While God *does* intend for each of his children to imitate Jesus and honor him with the body, he *does not* intend for each child to fulfill every possible good work. You cannot, and should not attempt to, meet every need in the world. So, the question becomes, "What is God leading *me* to do?" If you could wave a magic wand and do whatever you wanted to do for Christ and knew that you would be successful, what would you do? As you answer that question, you are well on your way to understanding the good works God has prepared for you to walk in.[19] In a world full of urgent need, let's take John Wesley's advice: "Do all the good you can, by all the means you can, in all the ways you can, in all the places you can, at all the times you

---

[18] Randy Alcorn, *The Treasure Principle* (Colorado Springs, CO: Multnomah Books, 2001), 17.

[19] Anders, 86.

can, to all the people you can, as long as ever you can."[20] Imagine how the world would change if every Christian lived like Jesus!

In possibly the greatest prayer in the New Testament, the writer of Hebrews prays, "Now may the God of peace...equip you with everything good that *you may do his will*, working in us that which is pleasing in his sight, through Jesus Christ, to whom be glory forever and ever. Amen" (Heb. 13:20–21, emphasis mine). In keeping with God's will, I pray you will "conduct yourselves in a manner worthy of the gospel of Christ" (Phil. 1:27). I pray you will "walk in a manner worthy of the calling with which you have been called" (Eph. 4:1). I pray you will "be steadfast, immovable, always abounding in the work of the Lord, knowing that in the Lord your labor is not in vain" (1 Cor. 15:58).

---

[20] The so-called "Rule of Wesley" cannot be found in his writings.

DISCUSSION QUESTIONS:

How would you explain the necessity of obedience in the Christian life?

Do you agree that most Christians in America are "educated beyond their obedience?" Explain.

What does it mean to love God with all your strength?

As we imitate Jesus, should we imitate *all* that he did? Explain.

How would you explain the relationship between good works and salvation?

Who should Christians do good works for?

What are some examples of good works?

What's the ultimate purpose of good works?

What role does the human body play in spiritual formation?

What biblical evidence do we have that the body matters?

What's the difference between spiritual disciplines and embodied disciplines?

Regarding good works, is it wrong to be motivated by reward? Explain.

7

CHAPTER

Formed for Mission: The Great Commission

Jesus came and said to them, "All authority in heaven and
on earth has been given to me. Go therefore and make
disciples of all nations, baptizing them in the name of the
Father and of the Son and of the Holy Spirit, teaching
them to observe all that I have commanded you. And
behold, I am with you always, to the end of the age."
– Matthew 28:18–20

Christianity without discipleship is always
Christianity without Christ.
– Dietrich Bonhoeffer[1]

I n the contemporary church, discipleship is often overlooked at
the expense of spiritual formation (or vice versa, depending on
one's denomination or Christian tradition). It's as if Jesus gives us
the option to choose *either* the Great Commandment *or* the Great

---

[1] Dietrich Bonhoeffer, *The Cost of Discipleship* (New York, NY: Touchstone,
1995), 59.

Commission.[2] Though many churches have practically disconnected the two, discipleship and spiritual formation are intrinsically united. Theology, at its best, should be understood and practiced as "whole person formation for mission."[3] Robert Mulholland Jr. explains, "No healthy spiritual formation is possible apart from mission with Christ. Similarly, no transformative mission with Christ is possible apart from formation in Christ."[4] In God's grand design, the Great Commandment and the Great Commission are reciprocal, fueling one another.

Rather than being an end in itself, spiritual formation naturally and inevitably expresses itself through the Great Commission. God works *in* his people in order to work *through* his people. Robert Mulholland Jr. expresses the necessity of mission in his definition of spiritual formation, stating spiritual formation is "a process of being conformed to the image of Christ *for the sake of others*."[5] Conformity to the image of Christ is conformity into a disciple-maker for the sake of others.

There is no more significant work for the Christian than the work of the Great Commission. The Great Commission is fulfilled through *discipleship*, which can be defined as *following Jesus and teaching others to do the same*. Discipleship is Jesus's plan A for expanding the kingdom of God, and there is no plan B. Unfortunately, there seems to be a discipleship deficit in the North American church. For a church to be deficient in discipleship is to be deficient in its

---

[2] Nathan A. Finn and Keith Whitfield, eds., *Spirituality for the Sent: Casting a New Vision for the Missional Church* (Downers Grove, IL: InterVarsity Press, 2017), 163.

[3] Jeffrey P. Greenman and George Kalazantis, eds., *Life in the Spirit: Spiritual Formation in Theological Perspective* (Downers Grove, IL: InterVarsity Press, 2010), 12.

[4] Robert Mulholland as cited in Finn and Whitfield, eds., 173.

[5] Robert Mulholland as cited in Evan Howard, *A Guide to Christian Spiritual Formation: How Scripture, Spirit, Community, and Mission Shape Our Souls* (Grand Rapids, MI: Baker Academic, 2018), 16 (emphasis mine).

primary reason for existence.[6] To ignore the Great Commission is to live in sin. The church must return to disciple-making as Jesus modeled and commanded.

Our understanding of mission should flow from our understanding of God himself. God is a missionary God, and the Bible is a missionary story. From Genesis to Revelation, God is on a mission to reconcile the world to himself (2 Cor. 5:19). God sent both his Son and his Spirit on a mission to the world. Jesus, who traveled the greatest distance (from heaven to earth) and made the greatest sacrifice, is the greatest missionary who ever lived.

Any depiction of Christian spiritual formation devoid of mission is inconsistent with God's character, Jesus's mission and teaching, and the Spirit's purpose. As the Father sent Jesus on a mission, so Jesus sends us on a mission (Jn. 17:18). In this final chapter, we will survey the Great Commission and the cost of discipleship. We will conclude by acknowledging God's presence with us and our responsibility to abide in Christ.

The Great Commission

A few days before Jesus ascends to heaven, he gives his disciples some final instructions. Today, we refer to those instructions as the Great Commission. As his last recorded words, the Great Commission expresses Jesus's greatest passion and top priority. The Great Commission is the only command of Jesus that is recorded in all four Gospels *and* the book of Acts (Mt. 28:18–20; Mk. 16:15; Lk. 24:46–47; Jn. 20:21; Acts 1:8). Jesus does not want his disciples to miss this command! Matthew records the Great Commission as follows:

---

[6] Eric Geiger, Michael Kelley, and Philip Nation, *Transformational Discipleship: How People Really Grow* (Nashville, TN: B&H Publishing Group, 2012), 11.

> Jesus came and said to them, "All authority in heaven and on earth has been given to me. Go therefore and make disciples of all nations, baptizing them in the name of the Father and of the Son and of the Holy Spirit, teaching them to observe all that I have commanded you. And behold, I am with you always, to the end of the age." (Mt. 28:18–20)

Jesus, the supreme authority of the church, has given the church its marching orders. When Jesus says, "go make disciples," his followers know exactly what he means because he had modeled it to them for three years. Jesus exhibits life-on-life discipleship as the most effective means to spread Christianity. He pours his life into the lives of his disciples and then tells them to go and do likewise. Jesus models life-on-life discipleship by inviting people into a relationship with himself, loving them, and showing them how to follow God.

The Great Commission is aimed at all followers of Jesus, both present and future. Therefore, every Christian should take personal responsibility for its fulfillment. JD Greear explains, "The gospel didn't advance in the early church through professional Christians and expert pastors; the gospel spread by the power of God working in and through the lives of normal people."[7] So, the question is not *if* we are called to fulfill the Great Commission, it's *where* and *how* we are to fulfill the Great Commission.

The primary command in the Great Commission is "make disciples." The words "go," "baptize," and "teach" all modify and explain how we are to make disciples. The Great Commission is fulfilled primarily through going, telling, baptizing, and training.

---

[7] J.D Greear, *Above All: The Gospel is the Source of the Church's Renewal* (Nashville, TN: B&H, 2019), 58.

Go

Jesus commands his followers to *go* on a deliberate quest to win nonbelievers to faith in him (Jn. 20:21,31). To *go* does not necessarily mean we must go far from home. The Great Commission technically says, *"As you are going,* make disciples." Though some Christians have a special calling to go to a specific place, Jesus assumes that everyday life will provide the context for disciple making.[8] For most people, everyday life includes marriage, parenting, friendships, work, and social life. All of these areas offer opportunities to fulfill God's mission. The overarching idea of the Great Commission is that whether we go next door or across the globe, Christians should be intentional and committed to the mission of Jesus. Like Jesus, Christians must take the initiative to pursue lost people.

Tell

Inherent to the command to *go* is the expectation to *tell* the gospel. Telling the gospel is referred to as *evangelism.* D.T. Niles famously described evangelism as "one beggar telling another beggar where to find bread."[9] As Christians, we herald Jesus as the bread of life (Jn. 6:50–51). Evangelism is inherent to Christianity because the gospel is the means by which God draws people to himself (Rom. 10:14–15). The goal of the Great Commission is to get the gospel to all nations. Jesus says, "this gospel of the kingdom will be proclaimed throughout the whole world as a testimony to all nations, and then the end will come" (Mt. 24:14).

Though we are imperfect vessels, Christians are stewards of the gospel (2 Cor. 4:7; 1 Cor. 4:1). Like Jesus, competent gospel stewards know, protect, *and* pass on the gospel. Jesus passed the gospel to

---

[8] Greear, 54.

[9] D.T. Niles, *That They May Have Life* (New York, NY: Harper and Brothers, 1951), 96.

his Apostles, and his Apostles passed the gospel to others who did likewise. Apostle Paul tells young Timothy, "what you have heard from me in the presence of many witnesses entrust to faithful men, who will be able to teach others also" (2 Tim 2:1–2). Paul later tells Timothy to "do the work of an evangelist" (2 Tim. 4:5). Because Timothy and others faithfully evangelized, the gospel made it to us! Now, our mission is to get the gospel to others, realizing the gospel came to us because it is headed to others.[10] Author David Bosch offers the church a helpful reminder regarding evangelism: "Evangelism is only possible when the community that evangelizes—the church— is a radiant manifestation of the Christian faith and exhibits an attractive lifestyle."[11]

Baptize

The third action the church must take to fulfill the Great Commission is "baptizing [new believers] in the name of the Father and of the Son and of the Holy Spirit" (Mt. 28:19). As we go and evangelize, God will draw people to himself (Rom. 10:17). Upon conversion, new believers should be baptized. Baptism does not save a person, but it does indicate one's willingness to obey Christ. Baptism expresses outwardly to the church what God is doing within a person. Through baptism, the new believer publicly confesses Christ as Lord and unites with a local body of believers. Every new convert needs a spiritual community to properly mature in the faith.

---

[10] Robby Gallaty, *Growing Up: How to Be a Disciple Who Makes Disciples* (Nashville, TN: B&H Publishing Group, 2013), xix.

[11] David Bosch, *Transforming Mission: Paradigm Shifts in Theology of Mission* (Maryknoll, NY: Orbis, 2011), 424.

Train

The fourth, and most neglected, action required to fulfill the Great Commission is to train new believers to observe all Jesus commanded. Notice that Jesus did *not* say, "Teach them all my commandments." Rather, he says, "Teach them *to observe* all my commandments." Discipleship involves more than the transfer of information; it involves ever-increasing obedience to all Jesus commanded. God's brilliant design for discipleship has built-in accountability because we must know and practice the commands of Christ in order to effectively train others to observe them. Disciple making is not complete until the disciple is practicing everything Jesus commanded, including the command to make other disciples.

By spending ninety percent of his time investing in a few men and commanding them to do likewise, Jesus modeled multiplication, not addition. In the same way we mature and reproduce on the biological level, God wants us to "be fruitful and multiply, and fill the earth" (Gen. 1:28; 9:1) on the spiritual level.[12] Thus, the mission of the church is not simply to add new converts but to make disciples who multiply. When new converts pursue the head, heart, and hands of Christ, they inevitably multiply.

The Cost of Discipleship

Jesus tells his potential disciples to "count the cost" of discipleship (Lk. 14:25–26). He says, "No one who puts his hand to the plow and looks back is fit for the kingdom of God" (Lk. 9:62). The call to discipleship is a call to deny ourselves, take up our crosses, and follow Jesus...no matter what. In response to Jesus's call, Peter and Andrew leave their nets (Mt. 4:19–20); James and John leave their boat, their family business, and their father (Mt. 4:21–22); and Matthew

---

[12] Kenneth Boa, *Conformed to His Image* (Grand Rapids, MI: Zondervan, 2001), 367.

leaves his lucrative tax business (Mk. 2:13–14). Jesus's original twelve disciples forsook safety, security, careers, comfort, families, friends, possessions, and even their own lives to follow him.

Jesus does not have two classes of disciples: those who abandon their lives to his service and those who do not. Though Jesus calls different disciples to different roles, the call to self-denial is the same for all. Jesus sometimes personalizes the cost of discipleship according to what he knows to be the priorities of a person's heart. For example, when a rich young ruler asks Jesus, "Good Teacher, what must I do to inherit eternal life?" (Mk. 10:17–22), Jesus knows the young man idolizes wealth. So, Jesus responds, "You lack one thing: go, sell all that you have and give to the poor, and you will have treasure in heaven; and come, follow me" (Mk. 10:21). Jesus's response devastates the young man because he realizes he cannot serve God and money (Lk. 16:13). The rich young ruler walks away from Jesus full of sorrow because the cost of discipleship is too high for him.

While the cost of discipleship is great, the cost of non-discipleship is much greater. By choosing earthly wealth over Jesus, the rich young ruler loses, among other things, the forgiveness of his sins, reconciliation with the Father, eternal joy (1 Jn. 1:3), the presence and power of the Holy Spirit (Acts 13:52; 1 Thess. 1:6), the benefits of being part of the church (Col. 1:18; Acts 2:42; 1 Jn. 1:7), and the provision of God's grace (2 Cor. 9:8; Phil. 4:19). As we see with the rich young ruler, losing God is the tragic reality for any person who refuses to follow Jesus in favor of worldly gain. Non-discipleship will cost a person the abundant life Jesus came to give.

Consider the paradox Jesus gives in Luke 9:24–25: "For whoever would save his life will lose it, but whoever loses his life for my sake will save it. For what does it profit a man if he gains the whole world and loses or forfeits himself?" Dying to self is the doorway to truly living. Losing oneself for Jesus's sake leads to finding oneself. Whatever a person may lose or "sacrifice" here on earth is not worth comparing to the eternal inheritance he or she will receive for obedience.

We all give our lives for something. If we are wise, we will leverage our lives for the sake of God's mission by following Jesus. When God brings history to an end, disciple making is the only mission that will matter. Greg Ogden states, "I can only hope and pray that a century from now (if Christ has not returned) when church historians study the time in which we live that it will be called an *age of discipleship*."[13]

God with Us

The Great Commission is primarily the work of God, who graciously allows us to participate with him. The Great Commission is a *co-mission* because Christians are on mission *with* Jesus. Jesus is at work all around us, and he invites us to participate with him. Divine-human synergy is the reality for our individual spiritual growth *and* the growth and expansion of the church. Jesus says, "*I* will build my church and the gates of hell shall not prevail against it" (Mt. 16:18, emphasis mine). Jesus claims all authority and all power (Mt. 28:18; 20). Still, Jesus commands *us* to go and make disciples. It's an awesome privilege to participate with Jesus to carry out the mission of God! The Great Commission is our "Great Privilege."

Realizing Jesus's power and presence, we should work diligently and confidently, knowing that as we obey, Jesus will build his church. Given the fact that God is with us as we obey him, we should accept that any deficiencies regarding the Great Commission are due to our lack of obedience. Jesus's last recorded words on earth are, "I am with you always" (Mt. 28:20). His last recorded words in the Bible are, "I am coming soon" (Rev. 22:20). The risen and returning Lord who was, and who is to come, is with the church now! Jesus is Immanuel,

---

[13] Greg Ogden, *Discipleship Essentials: A Guide to Building Your Life in Christ* (Downers Grove, IL: InterVarsity Press, 2007), 8.

God with us. The church is never left to do the work of God without the power of God.

The Distinguishing Mark of a Disciple Maker

The distinguishing mark of a Christian is love. Love should permeate the head, heart, and hands of all Jesus followers. Jesus says, "By this all people will know that you are my disciples, if you have love for one another" (Jn. 13:35). Without love, nothing else matters (1 Cor. 13:1–3). Love propels our pursuit of holiness, and love propels discipleship. To comprehend love correctly, we need to understand that love originates as a noun because "God is love" (1 Jn. 4:8). However, love is also a verb because God's love is actively displayed, primarily through Jesus. John, the "Apostle of Love," explains, "By this we know love, that he [Jesus] laid down his life for us, and we ought to lay down our lives for the brothers" (1 Jn. 3:16). Love is perfectly displayed by Jesus Christ.

The love of Jesus can be described as "willing self-sacrifice for the good of another that does not require reciprocation or that the person being loved is deserving."[14] Jesus's love is unconditional, sacrificial, and vulnerable. Jesus's love is genuine (Rom. 12:9), covers a multitude of sins (1 Pet. 4:8), seeks to serve rather than be served (Mt. 20:28), requires obedience (Jn. 15:9), requires discipline (Heb. 12:6), is sacrificial (Eph. 5:2), seeks to save the lost (Lk. 19:10), is patient and kind (1 Cor. 13:4), is not envious, arrogant, or rude (1 Cor. 13:4–5), does not insist on its own selfish way (1 Cor. 13:5), is not irritable or resentful (1 Cor. 13:5), rejoices only in the truth (1 Cor. 13:6), bears all things (1 Cor. 13:7), believes all things (1 Cor. 13:7), hopes all things (1 Cor. 13:7), endures all things (1 Cor. 13:7), and never ends (1 Cor. 13:8).

The love Jesus displays is the love he expects his followers to

---

[14] Paul David Tripp, *What Did You Expect?: Redeeming the Realities of Marriage* (Wheaton, Ill: Crossway, 2010), 188.

display (Jn. 13:34–35). As challenging as it seems to love like Jesus, we must remember that God supplies the power we need. Genuine love for God and others is part of the fruit of the Spirit (Gal. 5:22–23) and the fruit of abiding in Christ. As we walk in the Spirit and abide in Christ, our hearts are transformed, and we are able to love more and more like Jesus (Gal. 5:16).

Conclusion: Abide in Christ

As we pursue the Great Commandment and the Great Commission, we must realize the Christian life is not ultimately about doing things *for* Jesus; it's about abiding *in* Jesus. Jesus explains the essence of the Christian life in John 15:

> Abide in me, and I in you. As the branch cannot bear fruit by itself, unless it abides in the vine, neither can you, unless you abide in me. I am the vine; you are the branches. Whoever abides in me and I in him, he it is that bears much fruit, for apart from me you can do nothing. If anyone does not abide in me he is thrown away like a branch and withers; and the branches are gathered, thrown into the fire, and burned. If you abide in me, and my words abide in you, ask whatever you wish, and it will be done for you. By this my Father is glorified, that you bear much fruit and so prove to be my disciples. As the Father has loved me, so have I loved you. Abide in my love. If you keep my commandments, you will abide in my love, just as I have kept my Father's commandments and abide in his love. These things I have spoken to you, that my joy may be in you, and that your joy may be full. (Jn. 15:4–11)

We can do all things through Christ and nothing meaningful without him (Phil. 4:13; Jn. 15:5). As we pursue holistic holiness, we are able to increasingly live our lives as if Jesus were living through us, and that's just it; Jesus is living through us! Paul explains, "I have been crucified with Christ. It is no longer I who live, but Christ who lives in me. And the life I now live in the flesh I live by faith in the Son of God, who loved me and gave himself for me" (Gal. 2:20).

As you pursue holistic holiness, this is my prayer for you: "May God himself, the God of peace, sanctify you through and through. May your whole spirit, soul and body be kept blameless at the coming of our Lord Jesus Christ" (1 Thess. 5:23). May you "grow in the grace and knowledge of our Lord and Savior Jesus Christ" (2 Pet. 3:18). I pray you will abide in Jesus and bear fruit to the glory of God. I pray your joy will be full. I pray that when you fail, you will repent and press on, remembering that the perfection of Christ has been credited to you. I pray you will run the race with endurance and keep your eyes on Jesus, the founder and perfecter of your faith (Heb. 12:1–2). I pray you will fight the good fight, keep the faith, and finish well (2 Tim 4:7; 1 Cor. 9:24–27; Acts 20:24).

As we pursue holiness, our testimony should be the same as John Newton's, who said, "I am not what I ought to be. I am not what I wish to be. I am not what I one day will be. But, by the grace of God, I am not what I once was."[15]

---

[15] Tony Reinke, *Newton on the Christian Life: To Live is Christ* (Wheaton, IL: Crossway, 2015), 268.

DISCUSSION QUESTIONS:

How would you explain the relationship between the Great Commandment and the Great Commission?

Why is discipleship critical to Christianity?

Who is responsible for fulfilling the Great Commission?

How does one fulfill the Great Commission?

What is the cost of discipleship?

What is the cost of non-discipleship?

What does your lifestyle say about your commitment to the Great Commission?

What promises can we rest in as we participate in the Great Commission?

What is the distinguishing mark of a disciple maker?

What does it mean to "abide" in Jesus?